EMBRACING SOLITUDE

A Guide to Unlocking Greatness in the Process

Dr. Sandra Hill

EMBRACING SOLITUDE

Copyright @ 2023 Dr. Sandra Hill. All rights reserved.

No part of this book may be reproduced electronically or mechanically or photocopied or recorded, by a retrieval system, without permission given by the publisher.

All Scripture quotes are taken from the HOLY BIBLE. All other quotations were given permission from the author of those quotes.

Printed in the United States of America

ISBN: 979-8-9871235-0-8

DEDICATION

To those who have found solace in quiet moments, to the brave souls who have embraced solitude, this book of my voyage through solitude is dedicated to you.

In the stillness of your own company, self-introspection is an important part of self-awareness, and I also dedicate this book to help individuals searching to gain insight into their own feelings, responses, behaviors, pain, and grief.

There is strength gained from a greater sense of self, better relationships, and stronger decision-making skills. Also, there is power gained from inner peace, a profound inner calm that allows one to navigate the ups and downs of life with grace and resilience.

May these pages serve as a companion on your journey of self-reflection and growth, a testament to the richness of solitude, and a reminder that we are never truly alone.

With gratitude for your courage to explore depths of your own soul, while traveling with me. This book is lovingly dedicated to you!

ACKNOWLEDGMENTS

I stand at the threshold of this journey's end with a heart overflowing with gratitude. *Embracing Solitude* would not have been possible without God's Grace and Mercy toward me and the constant support and love of those who have been the pillars in my life throughout this wonderful season.

To my family, for your unconditional love, understanding, and patience, which have been my greatest blessings. Mommy, your love, peace, joy, wisdom, and prayers have been the guiding light along our pathway since birth. My sister Caron, thank you for being forever in unity with me. My precious children, Nicole, Nicholas, and Natasha, for your strength, patience, and thoughtfulness, which allowed me the space and time needed to begin healing and recording my grief journey through divorce, ultimately giving me a voice to pour out onto these pages. Thank you for selflessly allowing me to help others in the world. My precious grandchildren, Jayla, Jayce, Nazian, and Nalani, thank you for loving me unconditionally. Nana loves you more!

To my dearest pastor, Tony Page, a man after God's own heart, I honor you. Thank you for your fervent, effectual prayers, spiritual guidance, leadership, teaching, preaching, mentoring, coaching, and empowering. Thank you for seeing in me what I did not often see in myself. Your unwavering faith, love, discipline, determination, and obedience to God was the example that aided me to see this journey through to fruition. I also honor the men of God who preceded you: Bishop Victor Curry (FL), Dr. Ray VanderWal (Jacksonville Theological Seminary-FL), and Rev. Clyde Ellis (VA), who sowed seeds into my life that you immediately watered, and dug deeper holes to sow a different level of seeds, so I could become like a tree planted by the rivers of water, deeply rooted, to bring forth fruit in due season—so whatever I will do shall prosper. All for God's Glory! "Thanks" is not enough to express my depth of appreciation. I am SOOO grateful.

To Bishop Kenneth Chism-Restoration House, International, I am honored that you gave me permission to use your quotes and artwork as takeaways/ nuggets to share with my readers. Thank you for your kindness, sir.

To all the weekly PUSH prayer-line warriors at F2FWC and those throughout the nation, such as Fredericka Brown, Arstella Smith, and Camille McDonald, who have walked with me from the very beginning. And Elsie Cooper, Sheryl Adkins, and Anna Capehart have remained constant through more recent times. All your faithful intercessions are the wind beneath my wings. To the unnamed women and men whom I facilitate classes to currently in Alexandria, previously in Prince William, and Rappahannock Detention, VA, thank you for allowing me a glimpse into your "real time" solitude.

To Shawn Mason-Shawnee Shoots in the DMV, you have lent authenticity to my story. Thank you for your anointed gift of photography, which captured my freedom.

As I release *Embracing Solitude* into the world, I do so with a grateful heart, full of love and appreciation for each one of you (named and unnamed). This book is a testament to the power of prayer, faith, loss, hope, obedience, and determination.

FOREWORD

Solitude is often viewed from a negative perspective. Many people fear solitude because it forces them to confront their inner selves and face their thoughts and emotions. Dr. Hill in her masterful writing style provides us with a unique glimpse into this thing called solitude. Dr. Hill helps us understand that solitude is not meant to be a source of fear but a source of healing and growth. In Matthew 14:23 we see Jesus withdrawing to a solitary place to pray after feeding the five thousand. He shows us that solitude is a place of strength and rejuvenation. By enfolding solitude, we can confront our fears, find healing, and experience personal transformation.

Solitude allows us to disconnect from the noise and distractions of the world and connect with God on a deeper level. Solitude provides us with an opportunity to reflect, meditate, and listen to the voice of God. It is in these moments that we can find clarity, peace, and direction for our lives.

In this insightful book you will learn that embracing solitude does not mean isolating ourselves from others but rather creating intentional moments of stillness and silence amidst our busy lives. Luke 5:16 chronicles how Jesus often withdrew to lonely places to pray. We can follow His example by setting aside dedicated time for solitude each day. Whether it is through prayer, meditation, or simply being present in the moment, we can cultivate a habit of solitude that nourishes our souls and deepens our relationship with God.

Dr. Hill provides another lens through which we can view solitude; she describes it as a gift from God that allows us to find solace, strength, and spiritual growth. It is a process that releases one's greatness. It is in the quiet moments of solitude that we can truly encounter God and experience His presence. We are encouraged to accept solitude, but not perceive it as loneliness: The book distinguishes between solitude and loneliness. While loneliness is a feeling of isolation and sadness, solitude is a state of being alone that you choose and find enriching.

Dr. Hill shares her personal story of solitude and how it transformed her life and helped her to discover her true self and value. She encourages us to see solitude as a "journey of rediscovery" as she calls it. She unveils for us the revelation that solitude is not only a gift, but a catalyst for transformative growth along our spiritual journey. In the stillness of solitude, God molds our character, strengthens our faith, and equips us for the challenges ahead. It is in these moments of solitude that we can truly become more like Christ.

Solitude holds great meaning and power in our lives. It helps us build inner strength, resilience, and self-confidence. In solitude we gain a deeper appreciation for relationships, how to set healthy boundaries, learning to say "no" and prioritizing our alone time to maintain a healthy mental and emotional well-being. Dr. Hill teaches us that setting boundaries protects us from burnout and allows us the opportunity to recharge.

Prepare yourselves to be challenged, provoked, and recalibrated to see solitude as a place of healing and wholeness. Your perspective will be redirected, and your concept of relationships enhanced. Dr. Hill emphasizes the importance of surrounding yourself with people who support and uplift you. She helps us distinguish what quality relationships look like and how essential they are to our happiness and well-being. However, they should not come at the cost of your solitude.

I believe as you read Dr. Hill's story, you will experience an epiphany. An awakening of sort. You will see that solitude is the portal through which we all must go. It is the portal of self-discovery that releases us into the abundance of God's dream for each of us. In solitude we will experience the peace of God, which "surpasses all understanding that helps guard our hearts and minds."

It is my prayer that you will not see this book as just another book to read, and then place it upon your bookshelf as a task completed. I pray that this captivating work becomes a manifesto; a call-to-action that provokes you to do the work. To put into practice the instructions and principles Dr. Hill takes time to meticulously chronicle. It is my prayer that you will be better and begin thinking better so that your perspective concerning your singleness will be elevated to a revelation of your uniqueness and being a blessing from God. I hope it brings realization that you are not cursed or deficient but wonderfully and fearfully made in the image and likeness of God. It is my prayer that this book will usher you into the resting and loving arms of a Father who loves us and is concerned about every area of our lives.

As you heed the instructions chronicled in this book, know that God has made each of us a promise in Psalm 46:10. "Be still, and know that I am God." In solitude the opportunity to "know" God in a way that we have never known Him is made available. May we find comfort in the knowledge that God is with us in our solitude, guiding us and transforming us. My brother and sister, solitude is a gift from our Heavenly Father and a clarion call to rest in His love and allow Him to shape us into vessels of His grace.

Abundant Blessings, Dr. Hill, and thank you for presenting this testament of assurances that in the quiet and alone times of life, God has not forgotten us. He walks with us and talks with us and tells us His plan for our lives may involve times of solitude, with the solitude being the doorway to usher us into our GREATNESS!

Pastor Anthony X. Page, Face2Face Worship Center.

TABLE OF CONTENTS

FOREWORD.. i

INTRODUCTION 1

Chapter 1: THE JOURNEY OF SELF-REDISCOVERY 3

Chapter 2: HEALING FROM HEARTBREAK 13

Chapter 3: THE POWER OF SELF-LOVE 35

Chapter 4: REINVENTING YOUR LIFE 44

Chapter 5: NAVIGATING LONELINESS 49

Chapter 6: DATING AGAIN: A NEW ADVENTURE 77

Chapter 7: OVERCOMING RELATIONSHIP BAGGAGE ... 84

Chapter 8: INDEPENDENCE and PARTNERSHIP 91

Chapter 9: THRIVING IN SINGLENESS 98

Chapter 10: ILLUMINATING
FUTURE POSSIBILITIES 104

CONCLUSION 111

AUTHOR PORTRAIT: A TAPESTRY OF INSPIRATION 115

BOOKINGS, WORKSHOPS, CONFERENCES, FORUMS .. 117

RESOURCES 118

EMBRACING SOLITUDE: A GUIDE TO UNLOCKING
GREATNESS IN THE PROCESS 119

MEET THE AUTHOR: DR. SANDRA HILL 121

INTRODUCTION

Just when I thought I had settled into the most wonderful ride, life threw an unexpected twist my way, offering me a profound shift of self-discovery. I was becoming single again.

I was not a happy camper as I began my journey of solitude. I had to eventually choose to shakily surrender "again" to the Lord when He presented this writing assignment to me. He knew I could be trusted to carry it out to bless others, as I know that it is never about me. The pages you are embarking upon will be incredibly empowering as you extract your own identity, hidden talents, goals, and strengths that may have been overlooked while you were in a relationship that has now come to an end.

Descending into the depths of a roller-coaster ride of emotions, I encountered moments of fear and insecurity. I had questions about my worthiness, and the impossibility of ever loving again constantly haunted my thoughts. But these doubts are part of the solitude journey and should be embraced and confronted as opportunities for personal growth.

As the roller coaster ascended, I experienced a newfound thrill of independence. It is here that I realized I could conquer challenges on my own, make decisions without compromise, and define life on terms. This exhilarating sense of self-sufficiency has been one of the most rewarding aspects of the single journey for me.

For those who find themselves newly single, as the roller coaster ride hangs in the air and then nears its end, you may find yourself eventually open to the idea of love once again. This time, however, your approach will be with deeper understanding of yourself and your desires. You will have grown emotionally and be more attuned to what you truly seek in a partner. The prospect of love will probably become an exciting adventure rather than a source of anxiety.

The emotional roller coaster of being single again is a multifaceted journey filled with highs and lows, loops of loneliness, and unexpected twists and turns. It's a path of self-rediscovery, personal growth, and one with lots of potential. Therefore, embracing the ride, with all its emotional ups and downs, can lead to a very fulfilling and transformative experience. So, fasten your emotional seatbelt, and enjoy the adventure of this book as you rediscover yourself on the ride. Self-rediscovery is the compass that guided me toward a brighter and more fulfilling future.

In the pages that follow, I will share the intricacies of my learning experiences along the roller-coaster ride of singledom and delve into depths of emotions, navigate the challenges of letting go, and illuminate the possibilities that await. You are about to embark on a remarkable journey, one that will lead you to a deeper understanding of who you are and the incredible potential that lies within. As you turn the page and step forward, remember that the journey may be challenging, but the rewards are immeasurable.

Chapter 1

THE JOURNEY OF SELF-REDISCOVERY

"Knowing yourself is the beginning of all wisdom."
—Aristotle

The journey of self-rediscovery is not a linear path; it is a spectrum of emotions. We encounter grief, confusion, anger, and even sadness there. It is essential to acknowledge and honor these emotions because they are an integral part of the healing process. Just as we once celebrated love, now we must celebrate the courage it takes to face heartbreak head-on.

In the absence of a significant other, we may feel a void, a silence that was once filled with shared stories and shared dreams. It is natural to mourn the loss of that connection. However, in the very space left by that absence, there is an opportunity to reconnect with ourselves to rediscover our passions and to uncover the unique qualities that make us who we are.

Writing Our Own Story

This chapter is not negating the importance of relationships. It is about recognizing that our life's story does not begin and end with them. God is the author of our narrative, and this journey offers us a chance to rewrite our story with Him knowing and leading the way. It is an invitation to craft a life that is not defined by another person, but by God along with our own aspirations, dreams, and purpose.

Embracing solitude is not a lonely endeavor. It is an act of self-compassion, an investment in our own well-being, and an affirmation of our intrinsic worth. As we embark on this journey, remember that you are not alone; countless others have walked this path and emerged stronger, wiser, and more in tune with themselves.

Being single again can be akin to stepping onto an emotional roller coaster, complete with exhilarating highs and stomach-churning lows. After the end of a relationship, we often find ourselves on a solo journey of self-rediscovery and emotional turbulence. This roller coaster of emotions is a complex and sometimes bewildering experience filled with unexpected twists and turns.

The first sensation of being single again often resembles a thrilling skydiving free fall. The weight of commitments and compromises lifts, and you suddenly find yourself with a newfound sense of freedom. You can embrace spontaneity, make decisions solely for yourself, and rediscover your own identity. This initial high can be intoxicating as you revel with joy in the liberation from the constraints of a partnership.

As the roller coaster ascends, the initial excitement can give way to moments of loneliness. The void left by the past relationship can feel overwhelming, and you may find yourself yearning for the companionship you once had, Loneliness can manifest as a powerful emotion, but it is also a natural part of the single journey. It is during these moments that I reflected on what was lost and what I hoped to find in the future.

Life gets busy, and we can lose our authentic selves when we get caught up in relationships that are not or may not be good for us, or jobs we are not passionate about.

But why does self-discovery matter? Well, research shows that being connected to your true self is directly linked to your sense of meaning in life.

Feeling like your life has meaning can help you be happier and improve your overall well-being. Not to mention, getting in touch with your inner self will give you a better understanding of yourself. But the process of self-discovery is not easy. You will need focus, commitment, and a readiness to act.

Whether you're happy in your career or completely lost in life, there's no bad time to try out some self-discovery techniques. We can all benefit from a greater connection to our true selves. Let's dive into what self-discovery is and how you can get started.

What Is Self-Discovery?

Self-discovery is the process of learning more about who you are so that you can better recognize and understand your authentic self. You might already know what your core values are and your general likes and dislikes. Self-discovery goes much deeper than this, though.

Self-knowledge is crucial to understanding and regulating our emotions, personality traits, and behaviors. It gives us greater self-awareness, the ability to set better goals, and the potential to achieve personal growth.

Self-discovery is important because it allows us to look at our lives and determine what's missing.

Are you satisfied with yourself?

Knowing yourself means you won't need to rely on extrinsic motivation to move toward goals that reflect your personal values. As a result, you will be more likely to achieve them.

Self-discovery is an ongoing process. We won't find our sense of self scrolling through social media or buying new cars, clothes, or material things, even though I tried all that. Our journey of self-discovery will test our resilience and strength. It will also be meaningful, inspiring, and an excellent opportunity to grow.

Self-Discovery Techniques

Maybe you have already decided to gain some self-knowledge, but you don't know where to begin. Here's the thing: there's no correct way to go about this journey. It's yours! It is your journey.

If you find a technique that works for you but not others, it doesn't mean you're doing it wrong. Still, some self-discovery techniques might help you get in touch with your values and desires. Here are ten ideas I tried:

1. Consider your skills, gifts, and talents, no matter how big or small they are.
2. Get out of your comfort zone and try new things.
3. Think of your passions, interests, and dreams.
4. Spend time visualizing your ideal self and life, no matter how big or small.
5. Reflect on what you admire the most about yourself.
6. Journal your experiences, responses, changes, and thoughts.
7. Talk with a counselor, coach, or mentor for support.
8. Listen to podcasts or read inspiring books about other's journeys.
9. Do work to strengthen your mental health and well-being.
10. Follow your internal compass. Let go of other people's images and expectations of you.

The self-discovery journey doesn't necessarily require you to reinvent yourself (unless you want to). You can simply desire to understand yourself better. Maybe you want to be more in control of your life, or you feel a sense of urgency when planning your future.

You surely want to feel like you can accomplish your goals. You don't need to prove anything to anyone else during your self-discovery journey.

But when you show yourself that you can achieve your goals, your self-confidence and self-esteem grow. Plus, increased self-awareness can help you better identify potential obstacles to your goals.

A better understanding of yourself will also drive you to have healthier relationships. Increased self-awareness creates increased self-control, which can help you communicate better with friends, family members, and even coworkers. You will be able to offer sensible advice and honest options while regulating your emotions.

Remember, if you need extra support during your self-discovery journey, consider working with a therapist or counselor. A professional can help you stay focused, learn new self-discovery skills, and keep you from losing sight of your goals.

Questions to Ask Yourself on Your Self-Discovery Journey

To be yourself and identify what's missing from your life, you can always try asking yourself some questions. This is an important self-discovery technique.

Take a moment each day to pause and reflect. No one can do your self-exploration for you. Get comfortable, get rid of distractions, and get with your own thoughts.

Here are eight questions to ask yourself during this process:

1. What do you fear the most in life and why?
2. What lessons from your childhood have stuck with you to this day?
3. Does your job fulfill your needs and make you happy?
4. What problems are you facing now?
5. Do you make impulsive or well-thought-out decisions?
6. What's one thing you want to improve in your life, and how will you do that?
7. What are your top three values?
8. If you could do anything right now, what would you do?

Stages of the Self-Discovery Process

Self-discovery is an ongoing process that doesn't always feel good. Trust the process. You'll grow and change as you discover more about yourself. Your starting point will most likely feel nothing like the finish line.

As you move throughout the process, you may experience different stages. Throughout each stage, remember to take care of yourself.

Here are four stages of the self-discovery process and what you'll experience during each one of them:

1. Self-awareness
2. Awareness of interests
3. Awareness of dreams, ambitions, goals, purpose
4. Character / career discovery

Let's dig into a discussion about each step:

1. **Self-awareness**

This is when you realize your needs and acknowledge different personality traits, including your strengths and weaknesses. You may struggle with self-doubt here, but you can overcome it with resilience. Being honest about you are and what you want is crucial.

When you made mistakes in the past, how did you react? Is there a pattern?

2. **Awareness of interests**

Take note of your interests. What are your hobbies, likes, and dislikes? Is there a common theme? Narrowing down your interests helps you both personally and professionally.

Maybe the best part of your day is when you start making dinner. Bonus points if you're hosting a dinner party with all your friends. Do you enjoy the social aspect? Is the kitchen your safe place? What does that tell you about yourself?

3. **Awareness of dreams, ambitions, goals, passions, and purpose**

Daydreaming is okay—keep it in your schedule. You may experience plenty of it during your self-discovery journey. There is no limit on how many dreams you can have.

Once you know what you are passionate about and what it means to you, add more of it to your life, and more than likely you will bump right into your purpose.

These don't have to be career ambitions, either. You could register for a cooking class just for fun because you dream of being a better chef. Or you could plan a trip to a faraway country you've always wanted to visit. The sky's the limit.

4. Character / career discovery

After your list-making and planning, you might want to make a job change. All the hard work you put into narrowing down your interests, dreams, and goals will lead you to your true self. You might even identify your calling or passion in life and choose to pursue it!

Either way—congrats! You're getting in touch with your authentic self and what makes you happy. Now it's time to act upon some things you have learned about you.

Tips to Accept Yourself

Accepting yourself is an important step toward self-discovery. I found that it is impossible to learn about yourself if you turn a blind eye to things you don't like about yourself. If there is a struggle to see yourself for who you really are, it will be difficult to grow. If you are struggling with self-acceptance, and find yourself in a place of denial, here are some tips that may help you get to self-love:

1. Positive self-talk is a great place to start. Include it throughout your day.
2. Practice affirmations.
3. Love and embrace your weaknesses rather than try to hide them.
4. Take the challenging days as they come and know that they won't last forever.

5. Understand that your lifelong relationship is with YOURSELF.
6. Spend time alone, to get to know yourself better. You truly are never alone.
7. Accept the things you can't change about yourself and move forward.
8. Don't forget to laugh and find humor in your flaws! "A merry heart does good like medicine, but a broken spirit dries the bones" (Proverbs 17:22). Laughter is a gift from God. It can be a great way to stay encouraged.

The journey of self-discovery can be overwhelming! Self-reflection, self-reflection, self-reflection—it requires us to talk, and it oftentimes hurts because it is about difficult things. Share your thoughts with a trustworthy friend or family member.

There were many times I felt stuck or unsure about what my next move should be and had to discuss it with a trustworthy person. They may offer validation or confirmation of your pursuits, and of course they will make sure you are first in "prayer" about it all. I was fortunate most times to find a non-judgmental person in my life who would accept me for who I am and just observe and listen as I was going through the process.

Find yourself a supportive community that wants to see you accomplish your self-discovery goals, progress, and be successful through this difficult period of the journey. Get an accountability partner—someone you are checking in with, and they are checking in with you—as you discover your true self. Don't be surprised if the supportive person is not in church, although that is where we tend to look for that support.

"Strength is born in the moments when you think you can't go on but keep going anyway."
(Unknown)

Reflect & Pray

Loving Father, thank You for always being with me. Even though I don't know what may happen next, You do, and I trust You!

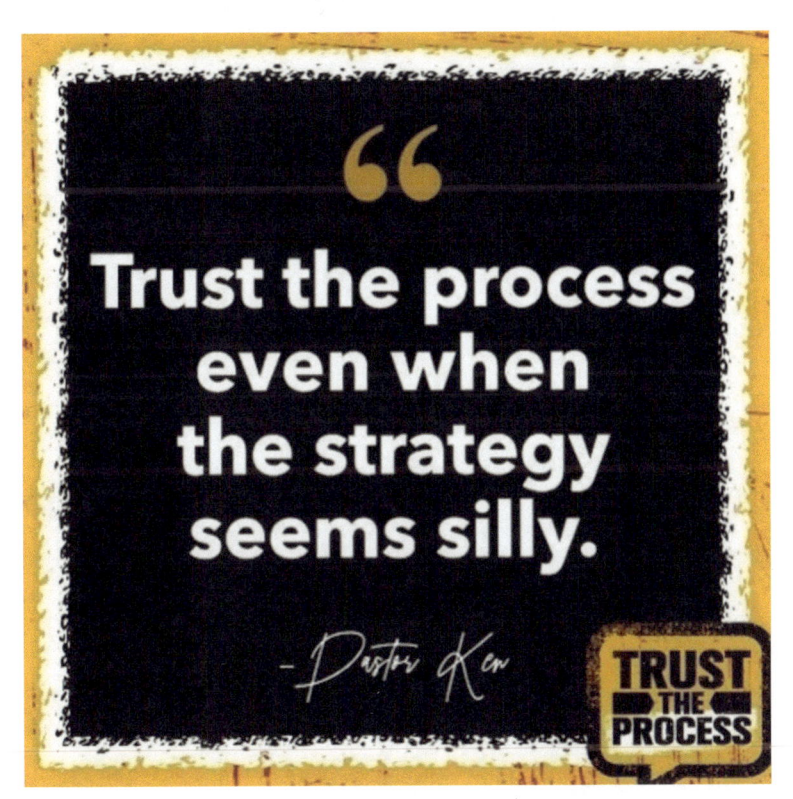

> **Trust the process even when the strategy seems silly.**
> — Pastor Ken
>
> TRUST THE PROCESS

Chapter 2

HEALING FROM HEARTBREAK

Healing from heartbreak can feel all-encompassing, like a storm that threatens to drown us in a sea of emotions. Healing for heartbreak is a pivotal step in our journey of embracing solitude, and it is a process that requires patience, self-compassion, and a willingness to face the pain head-on.

The Landscape of Grief

Grief is a natural response to loss, and a breakup is, undeniably, a profound loss. It's crucial to understand that grief is not a linear process with a fixed timeline. Instead, it's a landscape that we must navigate at our own pace. We may experience the stages of denial, anger, bargaining, depression, and acceptance, often cycling through them unpredictably. Allow yourself to feel and express those emotions without judgment.

The Importance of Self-Care

Healing begins with self-care. This is not just about bubble baths and spa days, although those can be wonderfully therapeutic. Self-care, in the context of healing from heartbreak, means prioritizing your physical and emotional well-being. It is about eating nourishing foods, getting regular exercise, and getting enough rest. It is also about seeking support from close friends, mentors, coaches, or advisers.

The waves of emotions that accompany heartbreak can be overwhelming. At times, I felt as if I was drowning in sadness, anger, or loneliness. Remember that these feelings are temporary, and like any storm, they will eventually pass. Journaling your thoughts and emotions can be a helpful way to process and release them, allowing you to gain clarity and perspective of what you are going through.

One of the most challenging aspects of healing from heartbreak is learning to let go. Letting go doesn't mean forgetting or invalidating your past experiences. Rather, it means releasing the grip of attachment to what was, and allowing space for what can be. This process can be painful, but I found that it was also liberating. It allows you to reclaim your autonomy and uncover the capacity for self-love.

Finding Meaning in the Pain

In the middle of heartbreak, it may be difficult to see any meaning or purpose in your path. However, as you progress through the healing process, you may begin to uncover valuable insights about yourself, your issues, and your past relationship(s).

Mirror, mirror on the wall, who is the fairest of them all? These insights can become steppingstones toward personal growth and resilience.

The Power of Forgiveness

Forgiving your former partner(s) and yourself is a vital part of the healing process. It doesn't mean condoning hurtful actions or excusing them; it means choosing to release the burden of anger and resentment.

Forgiveness is a gift you give to yourself, allowing you to be free in your heart from the weight of bitterness.

Embracing the Healing Journey

Healing from heartbreak is not a destination; it is an ongoing journey. There will be good days and bad days, moments of strength and moments of vulnerability. It is important to be patient with yourself and recognize that healing is a personal and unique process. Ultimately, it is a process that will lead you toward a place of greater emotional resilience, self-awareness, and self-compassion.

As we continue our path of embracing solitude, remember that healing from heartbreak is a testament to our inner strength and capacity for growth. It is a profound act of self-love, paving the way for the transformative journey that lies ahead. In the chapters that follow, we will explore how the healing process can prepare us to rediscover our true self and embrace the richness of solitude with an open heart.

Breakups, separations, divorces, and deaths are usually accompanied by intense emotional pain. The end of significant relationships can feel like a deep wound that needs healing in this journey. It is crucial to understand the pain we are experiencing and acknowledge its impact on our life.

The Initial Shock and Grief

The aftermath of a breakup can leave us in a state of shock and disbelief. This initial phase may be marked by denial and an overwhelming sense of loss. You may find yourself cycling through various stages of grief, including anger, bargaining, and sadness. It's important to allow yourself to feel these emotions and not suppress them. Some people I interviewed for this book who were going through divorce stated things like, "I find myself bursting out in uncontrollable crying bouts, which I never expected."

Practicing Self-Compassion

One of the first steps in healing is practicing self-compassion. Treat yourself with kindness and understanding during this challenging time. Understand that it is okay to feel pain, and it is a natural part of the healing process. Avoid self-blame and self-criticism, as they only prolong the pain.

Accepting the End of the Relationship

Acceptance is key to healing. It's important to acknowledge that the relationship has ended and you cannot change the past. Acceptance doesn't mean you have to like or condone what happened, but it's about coming to terms with the reality of the situation.

Seeking Support

Healing from a breakup, separation, divorce, or death is not a journey you should undertake alone. Friends (real ones) and family can provide invaluable support during this time. They can offer a listening ear, companionship, and a sense of belonging that helps you cope with the pain.

Therapeutic Support

Consider seeking professional help from a therapist, as stated before. Therapy provides a safe space to explore your emotions, gain insights into the relationship, and develop coping strategies. Therapists can also guide you toward healthier ways of dealing with the pain.

Self-Reflection and Growth

Taking time to reflect on the relationship can be a crucial part of healing. This doesn't mean dwelling on blame or regret, but rather gaining insight into what you have learned about yourself and your needs. Understanding why the relationship ended can help you grow and make more informed choices in the future.

Setting Personal Goals

Channel the pain into personal growth. Set goals for yourself, both short- and long-term ones. This can be a powerful way to regain a sense of purpose and direction in your life. Achieving these goals boosts your self-esteem and confidence.

Managing Emotions

Dealing with Anger and Resentment

It is common to feel anger, resentment, and pain with a breakup. These emotions can be intense and overwhelming. Finding healthy outlets for them, such as physical exercise, journaling, or talking to a professional, can be essential to prevent the emotions from festering.

Dealing with Sadness and Loneliness

Sadness and loneliness are common emotions during this time. Allow yourself to grieve the loss of the relationship. Engage in self-care activities, connect with supportive groups, and consider joining social or hobby groups to help combat the loneliness.

Reconnect with Your Passions

Use this time to rediscover your interests and passions. Reconnecting with activities you love can help you regain a sense of self and joy. It is an opportunity to focus on your own happiness and fulfillment.

Self-Care and Self-Love

Practice self-care and self-love. This involves taking care of your physical and emotional well-being. Exercise, eat well, get enough rest, and engage in activities that nurture your soul. Self-love is about treating yourself with the same kindness and respect you would offer to a friend.

Building Healthy Relationships

Learning from the Past

As you heal, it is essential to reflect on the lessons you have learned from your previous relationship. Understand what worked and what did not, and use the knowledge gained to build healthier relationships in the future.

Opening Yourself to New Connections

While healing, you may eventually consider opening yourself to new connections. This should be done at your own pace. Remember that each relationship is unique, and it is essential to approach it with a healthy sense of self and clear boundaries.

The Road to a New Beginning

Embracing a New Chapter

Healing from a breakup, separation, or divorce is a transformative journey. It's an opportunity to reinvent yourself, grow stronger, and find happiness in new and unexpected ways. As you get close to the end of this journey, you may discover that the pain has shaped you into a wiser, more resilient, and more compassionate person. Embrace the new chapter of your life with hope and optimism, knowing that you have the strength to face whatever lies ahead.

Healing from the pain of a breakup, separation, death, or divorce is a complex and deeply personal journey. It involves self-compassion, support from others, self-reflection, and personal growth. While the process can be challenging, it ultimately leads to a much better version of you. The pain may be a part of your history, but it doesn't have to define your future.

Rising from the Ashes

In the aftermath of heartbreak, we often find ourselves at a crossroads, faced with two paths: one that leads us down a dark, desolate abyss of despair, or another that offers a glimmer of hope, a journey toward healing. The choice is yours, but let me share some reasons why the latter path is the one worth taking.

1. **Embrace the Pain**: As counterintuitive as it may seem, healing begins with acknowledging the pain. It's okay to hurt, to grieve, to feel lost in the depths of heartbreak. You are not alone. We have all been there, and we have all risen stronger.
2. **The Power of Resilience**: Remember that within us lies a reservoir of resilience we never knew we had. Life throws its toughest challenges at us to reveal our inner strength. Heartbreak is another test.
3. **Rediscover Yourself:** Heartbreak provides a unique opportunity to reconnect with who you are. When you are no longer defined by a relationship, you can explore your passions, interests, and dreams without limitations.
4. **Surround Yourself with Support**: Lean on your support groups who genuinely care about your well-being. They will be your pillars of strength, your cheerleaders, and your haven during times of need. They should be individuals you discerned to be sent by God.
5. **Cherish the Lessons:** Every heartbreak carries invaluable lessons. It teaches us about love, about ourselves, and about what we truly deserve. Don't let these lessons go to waste.
6. **Forgiveness, Including Self-Forgiveness:** Healing requires forgiveness, both of the person who broke your heart and, perhaps most importantly, of yourself. Forgive yourself of any perceived mistakes or shortcomings.
7. **The Future Awaits:** As painful as it is to leave behind the past, remember that the future holds infinite possibilities—new relationships, new experiences, and a brighter chapter that is waiting for you to embrace it.
8. **A Stronger You Emerges**: When you emerge from the cocoon of heartbreak, you will find yourself transformed. The scars remain, but they serve as a reminder of your resilience and capacity to love again.

9. **Love Anew**: Do not let heartbreak close your heart or harden it forever. Allow yourself to love again, but this time with the wisdom and strength you have gained.
10. **Your Journey, Your Triumph**: Healing from heartbreak is a journey that is uniquely ours. It should not be about how fast we heal, but about the progress we make every day. It is about healing with a healthy mind. It is the triumph of the human spirit.

So, my dear friends, I challenge you to choose the path of healing. Embrace the pain, harness the resilience, and let the transformative power of heartbreak guide you toward a future filled with love, joy, peace, and a stronger, wiser you. The road may be challenging, but it is a journey worth taking to receive "beauty for ashes."

Learn to get up and get stronger when life knocks you down so you can get a lot more out of life. It's not the end; it is just a pothole along the journey.

I created a solitude journal during my healing time: We live in a world of constant challenges and obstacles. We all deal with sickness, trauma, tragedies, losses, and life's daily stressors, and it is all so unpredictable. Just when things feel manageable, something unexpected happens, and we start feeling anxious and overwhelmed again.

We can't change that life is hard, but we can learn to cope and adapt. We can also learn to change how we interpret our failures and disappointments so that it feels purposeful and perhaps even crucial for our healing and personal growth. That is why I created the journal, to get more out of life. It was developed with four sections, focusing on physical, emotional, mental, and spiritual exercises. The journal represents the holistic journey to fostering inner strength. It includes questions for reflection and both writing and doodling prompts. Its purpose is to help us create our own personal roadmap to resilience so we can change what we can and make the best of the rest.

Why Invest in the Journal?

1. You will begin to feel confident in your ability to handle life's challenges and adapt to the unknown. The questions and answers will help to identify your strengths and improve upon your weaknesses, so you feel prepared for the unexpected and capable of coping with whatever life throws at you next.
2. You will start seeing your struggles as opportunities for growth and be better able to find gifts in your pain. By reflecting on the good that has come from your struggle, you will start to see gains in your losses and strengthen and reframe your emotional muscles.
3. You will develop a greater sense of emotional awareness and feel less overwhelmed by your feelings. With one-fourth of the journey dedicated to emotional intelligence, I found a better understanding of my triggers and how to respond to them more skillfully.
4. You will be less apt to act out over-emotionally and say and do things you may regret. With a greater sense of emotional intelligence, you tend to develop the ability to evaluate your emotions (they will "sting" less) and you more than likely will pause before reacting.
5. You will identify the people and things that empower you and set boundaries to limit your exposure to the people and things that drain or exhaust you.
6. You will begin to recognize who and what gives you energy and what needs to change.
7. You will recognize how technology can hinder or help you. Instead of spending hours mindlessly swiping and scrolling, you will begin to use technology in a way that better supports your overall well-being.
8. You may decrease the odds of struggling with depression and anxiety.

Instead of being in a pit of despair, you can learn how to bounce back stronger than before. You can reduce your risk of excessive stress and protect yourself from a host of physical illnesses. The journal will help you to empower yourself, heal and find peace, and it started with one woman's journey—mine.

Many times, I was a fugitive from my feelings. Psychologists suggest that we are driven by two connected motivations: to feel pleasure and to avoid pain. Most of us devote more energy to the latter than the former. Instead of being proactive and making a choice for our happiness, we react to things that happen in our lives and fight or flee to minimize our pain. Oftentimes we stay and either avoid confrontation or initiate one to feel a sense of control. From a young age I felt overwhelmed by pain. As a pre-teen I ate my worrisome feelings. As a teenager, I started to starve my feelings away. And in my twenties, I felt that I cried my eyes raw. I sobbed and wailed, I convulsed and shook them up; I pushed my feelings down, one on top of another. At some point I had to begin learning to deal with my feelings, from events large and small. Little did I know that it was preparing me for such a time as this.

What I learned came down to three steps:

1. **Developing emotional intelligence**
2. **Learning to sit with negative feelings**
3. **Creating situations for positive feelings**

Emotional Intelligence

Researchers claim this idea is the missing link in terms of success and effectiveness in life. It didn't seem to make sense why people with high IQs and supreme reasoning, verbal, and math skills could still struggle in social and professional situations. It is stated that if you have a high emotional intelligence (EI), you likely regulate your emotions well, handle uncertainties and difficulties without excessive panic, stress, and fear, and avoid overacting to situations before knowing the full details. If you have low EI, you might be oversensitive to other people's feelings in response to them and obsess about problems until you find a concrete solution. In other words, you may feel bad far more than you feel good.

Some Steps to Improve Emotional Intelligence

1. **Understand what emotional intelligence looks like.**

Psychologist Daniel Coleman identified five elements to EI: self-awareness, self-regulation, motivation, empathy, and social skills. This means you understand what is going on in your head and heart, you don't make hasty decisions on impulse, you can motivate yourself to delay gratification, you listen to, understand, and relate to other people well, and you're able to focus on other people.

2. **Use meditation to regulate emotions.**

It's easier to deal with emotions as they arise if you've already done a little work to create a calm inner space. If you're new to meditation, you may want to try to make meditation easy and fun.

3. **Take an honest look at your reactions.**

Do you assume you know what other people feel and take responsibility for that? Do you freak out over stressful situations, blaming other people, being hard on yourself, and panicking over possible consequences?

4. **Practice observing your feelings and taking responsibility for them.**

It's not always easy to understand a feeling when it happens, especially if you think you shouldn't feel it, but forget about what you should do. Instead, try to pinpoint exactly what you feel—scared, frustrated, worried, ashamed, agitated, or angry—and then determine what might be the cause. Reserve judgment.

Simply find the cause and effect, i.e., I seemed unhappy with you when you did or said x, y, z, so I now feel stressed, or your significant other expressed dissatisfaction, so now you feel scared. Anytime you feel something uncomfortable that you would rather avoid, put a magnifying glass on it.

Once you know what you feel, you can now challenge both the cause and the effect.

You can ask yourself whether you're overreacting to the event or worrying to find a sense of control. And then you can accept that there is an alternative; you can choose to interpret the situation a different way, soothe yourself, and then feel something different. No one else causes our feelings. Only we can choose to change them.

5. **Learn to Sit with Negative Feelings.**

Even if you reframe a situation to see things differently, there will be times when you may still feel something that seems negative. While not every situation requires panic, sometimes our feelings are appropriate for the events going on in our lives.

We are allowed to feel whatever we need to feel. If we lose someone from our lives, we're allowed to hurt. If we hurt someone, we're allowed to feel guilty. If we make a mistake, we're allowed to feel regretful. Positive thinking can be a powerful tool for happiness, but it's more detrimental than helpful if we use it to avoid dealing with life. Pain is a part of life, and we can't avoid it by resisting it. We can only minimize it by accepting it and dealing with it well.

That means feeling the pain and knowing it will pass. No feeling lasts forever. It means sitting in the discomfort and waiting before acting. There will come a time when we feel healed and empowered to act. I don't regret much in life, but in retrospect, some of the most damaging decisions I have made have resulted from me feeling the need to do something with my emotions. I'd feel angry, or I'd feel ashamed. Our power comes from realizing we don't need to act on pain; and if we need to diffuse it, we can channel it into something healthy and productive, like writing, painting, or doing something physical.

Pain is sometimes an indication we need to set boundaries, or learn to say 'no" more often, or take better care of ourselves. But sometimes it just means that it's human to hurt, and we need to let ourselves go through it.

Create Situations for Positive Feelings

We tend to be more reactive than proactive, but that's often a decision we let the outside world dictate. We don't need to sit around waiting for other people to evoke our feelings. Instead, we can take responsibility to create our own inner world. We can identify what we want to say yes to in life and choose that before struggling with whether to say no to someone else. If you love dancing, take a class. If your greatest passion is writing, start a blog. If you daydream about being a musician, start recording. Don't worry about where it's leading. Do it just because you love it. For me, it is writing. It gives me a renewed sense of confidence. I always need more of that. We all need more of whatever it is. We need to do the things we love.

Negative feelings are only negative if they are excessive and many times continuing. We don't have to feel bad nearly as often as we think. If we choose to foster a sense of inner peace, challenge our perceptions and interpretations when our emotions could use some schooling, and learn to take responsibility for our joy, we not only minimize pain, but we can also choose to be a source of pleasure, for ourselves and the people around us.

The fragments of life that we may think are good for nothing or negative are sometimes food for giving. Our Master wastes nothing, and it just may surprise us and lovingly blend in with His healing joy and become our abundant wealth and overflow to others. Listen to the famous words from the Gospel of John:

"I am the true vine, and my Father is the gardener. He cuts off every branch in me that bears no fruit, while every branch that does bear fruit he prunes, so that it will be even more fruitful. Remain in me, as I also remain in you. No branch can bear fruit by itself; it must remain in the vine. Neither can you bear fruit unless you remain In me" (John 15:1- 2; 4-5 NIV).

You see, for the gardener it's personal, because we are the branches. His purpose is multifaceted, but restoration is the primary goal. The task is carried out in love, and incisions are made. Pruning of grapevines is always done in the winter while the vine is dormant. The aim is to selectively thin out any competing shoots or branches that show signs of disease or that may infect the surrounding branches. Left to their own, grapevines grow too dense with insufficient amounts of "fruiting wood," and the vine cannot breathe.

You know the feeling.

The gardener focuses on increasing fruiting wood but does not allow for too much fruit at the wrong time, which would cause the vine to lack the energy and nutrients needed to grow and fully ripen.

A secondary goal is to train the branches to grow on a structure conducive to harvesting and which conforms to the fence on which it grows, thereby establishing its future. Restoration pruning focuses on reestablishing a vine, particularly after a storm, to assure its recovery and strong springtime growth. The gardener is tender and strong at the same time; confident and decisive, and He knows the character and tendencies of each "portion" of his vineyard. It is so with us and with our grief.

You see, restoration gives back more than what has been taken. This is the victory!

Like the man in the synagogue in Mark 3 of the Bible, we stretch out our withered, grieving existence, and Jesus restores us. It is the nature of God's abundance and His restorative grace, which exceeds and runs over the boundaries of our grief because His love cannot be contained.

But first, there is pruning. No need to shy away. Listen: His pruning is His embrace, and all that is required is your consent. This is the meaning of "abide" in John 15. To be pruned is to retrain.

Some remnants, common to life and grief, have names you are familiar with, and they have stolen from you. Thus far you have not been able to remove their hold on your own. This is because the gardener has been waiting to do it for you, to restore you. I will give some of them a name, but you must be the one to present them to the gardener for pruning.

Whether your finger is pointing at yourself or at someone else, these must undergo pruning: resentment, anger, unforgiveness, bitterness, blame, regret, unwise or hurtful relationships, worldly vices, and false comforters. You may immediately know when you read the words if their presence has afflicted your mind and heart. They are bitter to the taste and defile your grief and your future. Yet you may have made a counterfeit peace with them. If you hold them near, they will taunt you and dishonor you.

My friend, the overflowing grace of each season is yours, and the promise of the gardener to restore you is sure, even if life feels permanently dormant now. The sacred fruit of your grief will thrive, and your roots will continue to grow deep and steady. Because for the gardener, remember, it's personal!

God not only reweaves what Satan incompetently intended for evil into good, but evil's attempts backfire so that in God's hands a glorious harvest emerges from what Satan had left for dead. What a gift!

Grieving Loss

God's breath, the ever-flowing life of His Spirit, will continue to develop in you. You will inhale and exhale again, without always catching your breath on the jagged edge of your pain. You will catch your breath, and you will live, because of your God.

Why It Hurts So Much

Some people describe loss, whether physical or divorce or breakup, as a tearing. Some say they can't breathe, and some say it feels like the bleeding won't stop. You know what they mean, because your loved one is gone or no longer there too. The bed that sometimes seemed too small for the both of you on a bad day, but never snug enough on a good one, now feels as vast as the ocean and bottomless as its deepest sea.

Your spouse is not there, and your heart feels like a dry wasteland. You never understood before, when others tried to explain it, but now . . . now you do. There is a "darkness" over the land for you too. The loss numbs your senses and inflames them all at the same time. When you look into the mirror of your memory, what gazes back is the weight and glory of that which your relationship reflected.

However, my friend, your pain now is temporal portion.

Look back into the reflective mirror of your relationship. There, springing forth from what you thought was a lifeless horizon, is a plentiful harvest of new life, violating death's assumed finality. Your grief is one of ineffable pain that requires a sacred response. The word *grief* cannot even begin to fully describe or contain it. In the same manner, Jesus' sacrifice for us was one of ineffable pain, requiring a sacred response as well, though words cannot describe or contain His pain either. But death doesn't make the rules. God does.

For you, my grieving friend, let the unknown be a time to rest your mind and body from their striving and find your repose in the arms of the one who inhabits the unknown. You see, "To have faith is to be sure of the things we hope for, to be certain of the things we cannot see" (Hebrews 11:1).

Settled

Maybe the Gospel writers used few words to describe the moment Jesus gave up His life because there aren't any words equal to the task. What words would have sufficed? Three hours of otherworldly darkness escorted the King to His death. And when His time had come, He cried out with a scream so unusual, so transcendent, and so powerful that the Temple veil tore, and the earth quaked and shuddered. The juncture at once declared history's preeminent triumph and unrivaled grief.

Whether there were dark hours leading up to your loss of relationship, you are familiar with the internal scream. Your world has quaked, and a seismic vibration now runs through the foundation of your life. But amidst all the crumbling and dust and buildup, the same God who created it all is the Rock of our salvation and can set us on a firm foundation.

I grew up in the Caribbean and Miami and have lived through earthquakes and tornados in both places. I know what it is to feel small and helpless and unable to stop the ground from quaking and the walls from closing in. But what I learned was that when our first home was built, it was important to begin with a foundation that would stand the test of time and any disruption. The contractor my dad enlisted for the task began the build in the middle of months that were cooler, and he had to pay special attention to the condition of the soil before setting the foundation in place. To support a structure the soil had to be settled, or the foundation would fail, and the home would be compromised. If the solid ground is disturbed, great care must be taken to compact it again before building. Much depends on the magnitude of the disturbance and severity of weather patterns in the surrounding area. The greater the shifting of soil, the greater the time needed to level it and make it suitable for building.

Grief has shifted the soils under the foundation of your life, my friend, and there is so much to consider. The disturbance underneath requires time to settle. Let it settle, because the future stability of what you build depends on how well the ground around your life comes to rest. Rushing through this period of settling will be detrimental.

Just like the intentional planning for a foundation, take intentional time to grieve. Do not bury the debris of your grief below the surface; it will degrade over time, and your house will shift and crack. Be patient; God will sift it for you. And while you wait, stay inside His love, where everything you need for healing is within reach.

Do not stand on the world's foundation, where the weather is inclement and seeks to draw you to compromise. Your physical health, relationships, emotions, and spiritual well-being must rest on the one true foundation, the Balm of Gilead who makes the wounded whole. Do not look elsewhere to false comforts where temporary relief is the counterfeit goal. Let grief settle and you will not sink under its weight. God will press the earth firmly around your roots, and you *will* stand . . . but give it time. He "Himself will restore you, make you strong, firm and steadfast" (1 Peter 5:10 NIV).

Grief requires tender and consistent care with each stage of life, and such is the loyalty of grief.

Refining metal with fire is one of the oldest methods known to humanity and is still in use today. Research shows that flames need to reach over 1,000 degrees Celsius for waste to rise to the top, but there is no loss in value to the remaining gold throughout the process, only increase in its worth and potential. Dross/waste is considered a contaminant and must be removed, or the value of the precious metal will be lost. To "refine" something literally means to free it and to improve it for the purpose of excellence. In Greek it translates "to be ignited." Fittingly, the symbol for gold (Au) comes from a Latin word meaning "shining or glowing dawn," because during the final stages of refining, the gold experiences what is called a "brightening." This phenomenon occurs when the last impurities vanish, and the pure metal emits a bright flash of light.

We don't miss the dross at all. It is made up of useless waste, and it keeps a broken heart from healing. Leaving it behind has never seemed painful, nor does it induce more grief, because the master's hand does the work of it and sees to its completion.

My persevering friend, the only comfort you may have right now are the tears on your face; and when you look forward, the seeming endlessness of it all appears to hold no hope for the future. Passions and dreams may have ended in your backyard, and memories may haunt instead of healing. But the compassionate flame of our Refiner will not leave us with riches that cannot be used. His love will not allow waste to tarnish your worth or potential. The treasure of your grief will remain to accomplish its purpose, but what is useless, what will not produce anything of value, and what will contaminate your future must be entrusted to the refining hand of God.

You cannot separate the dross yourself; it is too difficult. But that's okay. Everything is difficult right now, so one less thing to handle is a relief, a kind of healing in itself. The refining will continue throughout the life of your grief, but when it has been tried, you will come forth as gold. In God's providence, to be refined and live without the dross of grief means to be free, to be improved, and to be excellent.

"But He knows the way that I take. [and He has concern for it, appreciates, and pays attention to it.]. When He has tried me, I shall come forth as [refined] gold [pure and luminous]" (Job 23:10 AMP).

Remembering

Theologian Victor Shepherd said to remember "is to bring up a past event into the present so that what happened back then continues to happen right now. What unfolded back then, altering forever those whom it touched, continues to be operative now, altering those who 'remember' it now."

Think back, though. There is another event that contradicts the well-meaning intentions of our loved ones who misunderstood and wanted us to "move on" and "have more faith." It is the *altar of remembrance* that marks God's faithfulness and unrivaled power and stops at nothing to make a way for His people. This altar reminds us of when Jesus refused to save Himself so that He could save us from the unrelenting darkness. It invites us to trust when the path is covered in shadow and fear. That altar reminds us of when He brought us through the impossible and steadied us during chaos and future unknowns. It tells our story. This altar reminds us of God's promise to always be with us. This altar has boundless possibilities and the power to heal and transform our pain.

This altar *alters us forever,* as it should.

Grief must move and be expressed to be healthy, but we never simply "move on." Life is too sacred for that. No matter what anyone may tell you, dear friend, remembering is an expression of faith, when surrendered to God as an act of worship.

"Blessed are those who mourn, for they shall be comforted" (Matthew 5:4). Mourning is the intense experience and expression of grief. To get to the comfort, we mourn. It is here, at the altar of remembrance, that the blessing awaits, and that spiritual muscle is formed in faith and pain. This altar gives permission to grieve and remember. Your loss is worthy of the effort by far, and though it's hard to imagine, the comfort you receive will surpass the grievous night you inhabit now.

Dear grieving friend, you are free to remember, because God remembered you on the supreme altar of remembrance, and He asks us all to remember Him in return. He gets it. He understands.

Restoration

It's the middle of winter as I continue to complete this book, though it may not be that season for you, no matter what time of year it is. There is a certain chill that tarries with grief, despite the season. But there are other truths that accompany the ever-changing climate of grief, each as certain as the dawn and the shifting of the sun and rotation of the earth. It is our God who changes the seasons, and it is He who can restore in the middle of your winter, summer, or fall.

Our word "goodbye" literally comes from "God be with you." Other cultures have their own goodbye rituals.

For most of us, saying goodbye seldom feels good, but when we put God into the picture, when we insert His unfathomable name into the goodbye and dare to believe, perspectives change. No goodbye can separate us from the hope and promise of tomorrow.

As I stated before, God not only repairs the holes, tears, and damages that Satan incompetently intended for evil into good, but causes the attacks to backfire so that in His hands, stitch by stitch, He replicates our original structure, rendering the damaged areas undetectable, yielding his fearfully and wonderfully made child alive from being left for dead by Satan. What a gift!

Hold fast, my friend. Look up. God is nearby. I'm praying you through. It is the "good" in your goodbye that develops you in solitude. Your grief will continue to teach and minister as you abide and uncover your treasure. You have already begun to discover the miracle of the horizon, and I'm honored to be walking with you. I slid out from under the blanket of the past, and you can too. God will do more than heal your broken heart.

Your resilience is your greatest superpower. Have no fear.

Reflect & Pray

What are you fearing?

Father, thank You for being with me. I can trust You in those moments when my heart is overwhelmed, to see me through by Your Grace.

"You have not given me a spirit of fear, but of power, love, and a sound mind" (2 Timothy 1:7).

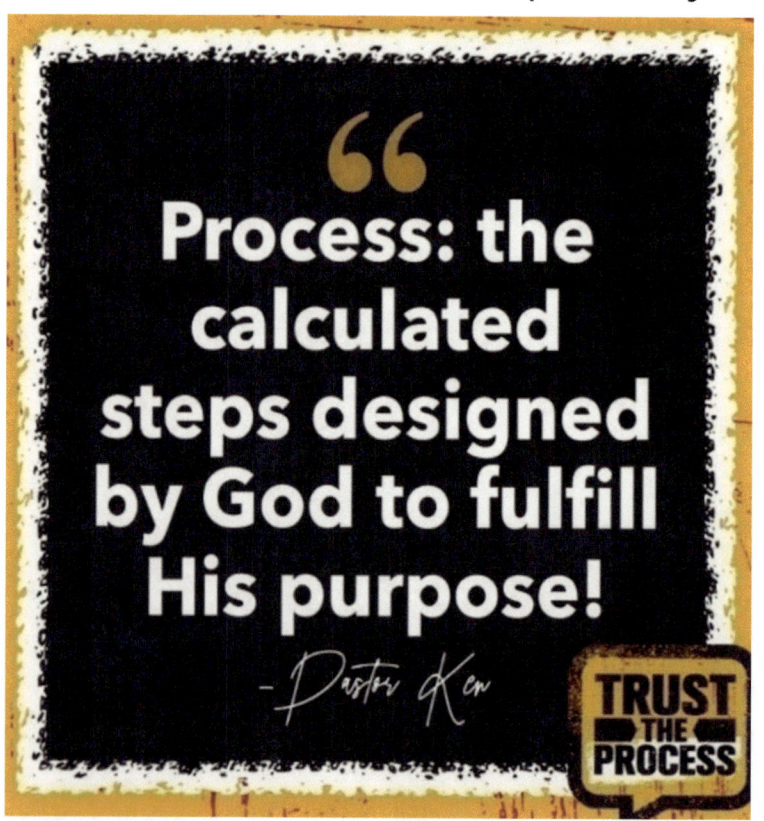

> "Process: the calculated steps designed by God to fulfill His purpose!
> — Pastor Ken
>
> TRUST THE PROCESS

Chapter 3

THE POWER OF SELF-LOVE

The Power of Self-Love

As you journey through the process of embracing solitude, you'll encounter a potent force that can heal wounds, build resilience, and illuminate your path of self-love. In the wake of a breakup, it's easy to lose sight of your worth, but in this chapter, we'll explore the profound transformation that can occur when you choose to love and care for yourself unconditionally.

The Foundation of Self-Love

Self-love is not a frivolous concept; it's the bedrock of a healthy and fulfilling life. It starts with recognizing your inherent worthiness, regardless of external circumstances or the opinions of others. This foundation allows you to navigate life's challenges from a place of inner strength and self-assuredness.

Understanding Self-Love

Self-love means recognizing your worthiness of love, respect, and care. It involves treating yourself with kindness. It is the belief that you deserve happiness, success, and fulfillment in your life.

Nurturing Self-Compassion

Self-compassion is an essential component of self-love. It involves treating yourself with the same kindness and understanding that you would offer a dear friend in times of distress. Embrace the practice of self-compassion during moments of self-doubt or when you make mistakes. Understand that you are human, and imperfection is a part of the human experience.

Self-compassion consists of three main components: self-kindness, common humanity, and mindfulness. Self-kindness involves being gentle and nurturing toward yourself. Common humanity reminds you that suffering is a universal human experience. Mindfulness encourages you to approach your pain with awareness.

Self-compassion is a powerful tool for nurturing self-love. When you treat yourself with compassion, you reinforce the belief that you are worthy of love and care. Self-compassion can counteract the inner critic and foster a more nurturing inner dialogue.

Letting Go of Self-Criticism

In the aftermath of a breakup, it is common to engage in self-criticism and blame. You might replay past events, questioning your choices and actions. However, self-criticism only perpetuates suffering. Instead, focus on self-reflection as a means of growth, not self-lashing. Use your past experiences as lessons to shape your future positively.

The Mirror of Affirmations

Affirmations are powerful tools for cultivating self-love. Create a list of positive statements about yourself and your worth. Repeat these affirmations daily to counteract negative self-talk. Over time, these affirmations can help reshape your self-perception and boost your self-esteem.

Affirmations that Ignite Your Self-Love Flame

- "I am worthy of love and happiness."
- "My self-worth is not determined by external circumstances."
- "I embrace my imperfections; they make me unique."

- "I am resilient, and I will emerge from this stronger than ever."
- "I choose to forgive and release what no longer serves me."
- "I am deserving of all love and joy that life has to offer."

Practicing Self-Care

Self-love extends to the care of your physical and emotional well-being. Engage in activities that nourish your body and soul, whether it's taking leisurely walks in nature, enjoying your favorite hobbies, or indulging in restorative self-care rituals. Prioritize your own needs and make self-care an integral part of your daily routine.

Setting Healthy Boundaries

Seeking and maintaining healthy boundaries is a critical aspect of self-love. Boundaries define what you're willing to accept in your relationships and interactions with others. Loving yourself means setting and maintaining healthy boundaries in all areas of your life. Boundaries protect your emotional well-being and ensure that you're treated with respect and dignity. Learn to say "no" when necessary and communicate your needs assertively and kindly. Healthy boundaries foster respect for yourself and teach others how to treat you.

Self-Doubt

Self-doubt is a common obstacle on the path of self-love. It manifests as the inner voice that questions your abilities, worth, and potential. Overcoming self-doubt is essential for building self-esteem and self-love.

Celebrating Your Achievements

To combat self-doubt, it's important to recognize and affirm your abilities and accomplishments. Keep a record of your achievements. Acknowledge and celebrate them, no matter how small they may seem. These victories are proof of your capabilities and strengths. By recognizing your accomplishments, you reinforce your self-worth and build confidence in your ability to face challenges.

The Freedom of Self-Love

Self-love is the key that unlocks the door to personal freedom and fulfillment. When you love and accept yourself unconditionally, you are no longer dependent on external validation for happiness. You understand who the architect of your life is, and that God is shaping it according to His will. He is the potter, and we are the clay.

The Evolving Journey of Self-Love

The Ongoing Process

Self-love is not a destination; it is an ongoing journey. Your relationship with yourself will evolve over time. Embrace the idea that self-love can deepen and grow as you continue to learn, change, and adapt.

Self-Worth and Its Importance

Self-worth is closely tied to self-love. It's the belief in your intrinsic value as a human being, regardless of external factors such as achievements, appearances, or others' opinions. Recognizing your self-worth is fundamental to building self-love.

When you have a strong sense of self-worth, you're less likely to seek validation from others. You make decisions based on what aligns with your values and desires, rather than trying to please others or conform to external expectations.

Your Inherent Value

In the journey of self-love, forgiveness, self-compassion, self-worth, and value are interconnected aspects that guide our paths to a more fulfilling and authentic life. In the grand tapestry of healing, self-love is the radiant thread that weaves through the darkest of moments, illuminating our path with its unwavering warmth and steadfastness. It is a transformative force that propels us toward a place of inner strength and unshakeable self-affirmation. Remember that self-love is not selfish; it's the foundation upon which we can build deeper, more meaningful relationships with others and a greater sense of purpose and fulfillment in our own life.

Self-Love: The Healing Elixir

Self-love is not a luxury; it is a necessity. In times of my heartbreak, I easily forgot my own worth. We pour our love into others, often neglecting the most important person—ourselves.

Self-love also means looking in the mirror, not to scrutinize perceived flaws, but to celebrate the beautiful, resilient soul that gazes back at you. Self-reflection allows you to grow, evolve, and become the best version of yourself.

Our inner voice should be our greatest ally, not our harshest critic. Replace self-criticism with self-compassion. Speak to yourself as you would to a cherished friend, with kindness and understanding.

Resilience, Rooted in Self-Love

When you love yourself unconditionally, you become resilient in the face of adversity. Heartbreak may have shaken you, but it cannot break you. You are the embodiment of strength, courage, and grace.

Embracing Your Magnificence

In your journey of self-love, remember this: You are a masterpiece in progress.

Your heartbreak does not define you. It refines you. You are a beacon of light, radiating warmth and love into the world.

A Love That Heals All

In the previous chapter of healing, self-love is the hero that ultimately saves the day. It's the balm that soothes the wounds, the light that guides the way, and the affirmation that you are enough, just as you are.

Dear reader, as you embark on this transformative journey of self-love, hold your head up high, and repeat after me. "**I am worthy. I am strong. I am loved**." With each affirmation you strengthen the power of self-love within you, and in doing so, you set yourself on the path to true healing and radiant self-transformation.

When we start gifting love to ourselves and not just to others, we are able to become more spiritually, mentally, emotionally, and physically empowered. Our best self steps forward and allows us to be totally open to the world and the people around us.

Sometimes, the act of flexing that self-love muscle is easier said than done.

When you tap into true self-love and acceptance, then all desires you have for yourself come from a place of choice, not fixing. And it all starts with unconditionally loving and accepting yourself, where you are right now, as you are learning now.

It's that simple.

Remember, as an individual who is gifted, passionate, and determined, a person of strength and value, just like you so freely express love to others, so, too, should you be with yourself. Life is full of balance, and it is our duty to put ourselves in the way of beauty; to create light when you are unable to find it. Through all the high tides and all the low, life is, and always will be, a beautiful journey.

The reality is this: when you like yourself, respect, care, and nurture yourself, when you believe you really do deserve love, pleasure, and to receive what you desire, then life gets sweeter.

It's an inward journey and there are no quick fixes, but it really is worth it.

Opening up the Heart

One of my favorite ways I began my yoga self-love mantra was with the opening heart ritual. Whenever I practiced this, I felt so at peace with myself, and I had this wonderful sensation, like I could take on the world! With commitment and consistency, you will fully feel the transformative power of this practice.

1. Find a quiet and calm space. Visualize your heart and relax your body.
2. Dab a little oil on your skin, just over the area on your chest where your heart is. Lavender or botanical extracts will help open and balance the heart and bring peace. Breathe in the nourishing scent deeply.
3. Next, visualize your heart.
4. Slow your breathing and calmly close your eyes, meditating on what you are grateful for.
5. As you breathe, visualize a flowing to your heart. Enjoy feelings of peace, love, and happiness.
6. When you're ready, slowly come out of breathing, opening your eyes and taking in everything around you with a fresh outlook. Notice the space you have just created within yourself. Just notice.
7. Repeat the mantra: "I am love. I let love in. I am kind to myself. I live in peace and gratitude."

Today I am a work in progress, but I can truly say I love the person I am becoming. The scars of my past are no longer defining me as much. They are a testimony of my resilience. My journey of some traumatic feelings to transformation is a change to self-love, self-acceptance, and strength that lies within me to overcome even the darkest of shadows. I am walking with newfound purpose, self-awareness, and deep abiding love for me and the person I was created to be.

Take a step, whether it is to seek therapy, share your story, or find a mentor or coach. Know that your journey is worth it. It helps us to inspire ourselves and others to personal growth and self-love. Our journey matters and our voice matters.

*You are not alone on this journey;
you have yourself.*

Reflect & Pray

Father, thank You for leading me and guiding me to a more fulfilling life. You surround me with a shield of protection.

I love you, Lord!

" I praise you because I am fearfully and wonderfully made; your works are wonderful; I know that full well" (Psalm 139:14).

> "The Process is as important as the destination!"
> — Pastor Ken
>
> TRUST THE PROCESS

Chapter 4

REINVENTING YOUR LIFE

In the aftermath of a breakup, you may find yourself standing at a crossroads, with the past behind you and a blank canvas of the future ahead. This chapter explores the exciting and transformative process of reinventing your life as you embrace the journey of being single again.

The Canvas of Possibilities

Imagine your life as an empty canvas, waiting for you to paint your dreams, desires, and aspirations. The end of a relationship doesn't signify the end of your story but rather the beginning of a new chapter, one that you get to design.

Embracing Change

Reinvention involves change, and change can be uncomfortable. It's essential to recognize that growth often occurs outside of your comfort zone. Be open to new experiences, even if they initially feel daunting. They may lead you to uncharted territory filled with unexpected joys.

In the chapters ahead, we will explore how this reinvention process can lead to personal empowerment, increased self-awareness, and a deeper appreciation of the solitude you've chosen to embrace. Remember, your life is a masterpiece in progress, and each stroke of the brush brings you closer to a future filled with promise and fulfillment. The Bible states in Ephesians 2:10, "We are God's masterpiece…" and God is no amateur potter, but one that has already begun to shape us into a masterpiece. He knows the potential in us that we cannot even grasp or truly understand.

The Opportunity for Reinvention

Embracing change with an open heart and a positive mindset is the first step toward reinvention. By recognizing the possibilities that come with being single, you can embark on a transformative journey.

Overcoming Fear and Uncertainty

Addressing Fear and Doubt
Reinvention often involves stepping into the unknown, which can be frightening. Address your fears and doubts by acknowledging them and reframing them as opportunities for growth.

Building Resilience
Building resilience is essential when facing uncertainty. Develop coping strategies, embrace change as a chance to learn and adapt, and draw strength from your past experiences of overcoming challenges.

Exploring New Opportunities

Openness to New Experiences
Be open to exploring new opportunities and experiences. Say yes to things you might have previously declined. New experiences can bring fresh perspectives and enrich your life.

Professional Growth
Consider how your professional life aligns with your reinvention goals. Explore new career opportunities or take courses to develop new skills. Your career can be a significant part of your journey toward transformation.

Learning from Past Relationships

Reflecting on Past Relationships
Take time to reflect on past relationships. Understand what you've learned about yourself, your needs, and your desires. Use these insights to make more informed choices in future relationships.

Celebrating Progress and Milestones

The Importance of Celebrating
Celebrate your progress and milestones again, along the way. Remember, acknowledge your achievements, no matter how small they may seem. Celebrations reinforce your commitment to positive change.

Staying Motivated
Use celebrations as a source of motivation. When you recognize your successes, you're more likely to stay dedicated to your reinvention journey.

Embracing a Fulfilling New Chapter

Reinventing your life and embracing positive change when you find yourself single again is a journey of self-discovery, growth, and transformation. It's an opportunity to create a life that aligns with your true self, values, and aspirations. Embrace change with an open heart, nurture self-love, set meaningful goals, and celebrate your progress along the way. Remember that the power to shape a fulfilling new chapter of your life lies within you, and your journey of reinvention is a testament to your resilience and capacity for growth.

One Day at a Time, Sweet Jesus

Life's challenges can be overwhelming but remember the wisdom of taking it one day at a time. Each day is a chapter in your healing journey. Focus on the present, and let the future unfold naturally.

Your Life, Your Masterpiece

Just as a painter breathes life into a canvas, you breathe life into your own existence. Your life is your masterpiece, and every moment is an opportunity to add vibrant colors, intricate details, and layers of meaning.

New Relationships, New Connections

As you reinvent your life, you'll also open yourself up to new relationships and connections. These may not replace what was lost, but they can enrich your journey and bring unexpected joy.

Every Ending Is a New Beginning

In the grand symphony of life, every ending is followed by a new beginning. Your heartbreak is not the end of your story; it's a poignant pause before the crescendo of a beautiful new chapter.

Dear reader, as you embark on this journey of reinvention, remember that you have the power to shape your destiny. Embrace change, set new goals, discover your authentic self, and take it one day at a time. With each step forward, you are creating a life that reflects your inner strength, resilience, and the boundless potential for happiness and fulfillment.

From every ending, a new beginning emerges.

Reflect & Pray

*Father, as I see and experience pain and need,
Loving God, soften my heart
to respond with compassion.*

"Create in me a clean heart, O God; and renew a right spirit within me" (Psalm 51:10).

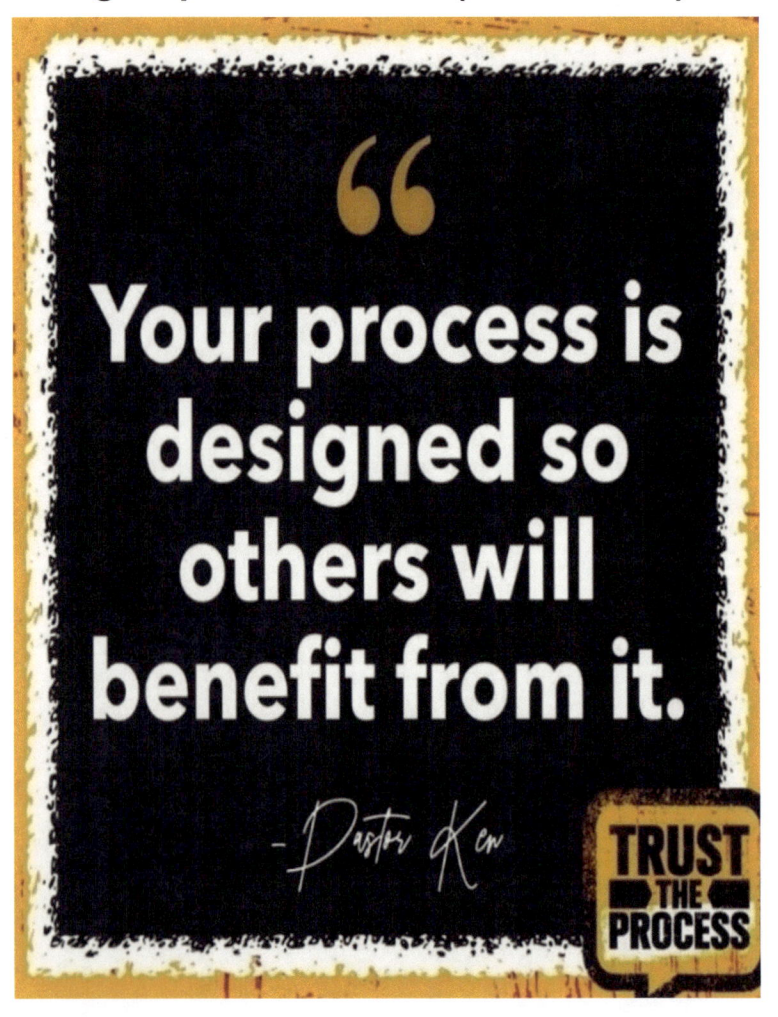

> **Your process is designed so others will benefit from it.**
> — Pastor Ken
>
> **TRUST THE PROCESS**

Chapter 5

NAVIGATING LONELINESS

Loneliness can be one of the most challenging aspects of being single again. It is a feeling that can creep in, making you question your decision to embrace solitude. However, loneliness is not your enemy; it's a messenger, inviting you to explore its depths and find the hidden treasures within.

The Paradox of Solitude

Solitude and loneliness may seem like two sides of the same coin, but they are distinct experiences. Solitude is a choice, an intentional embrace of being alone. Loneliness, on the other hand, often feels imposed and unwelcome. To navigate loneliness effectively, it's important to distinguish between these two states.

Understanding Loneliness

Loneliness is a universal human experience. It's not a sign of weakness or inadequacy; it's a natural response to the absence of social connection. When you're single again, it's common to feel a sense of loss and isolation. Acknowledging these feelings is the first step toward understanding and addressing them.

Embracing Solitude's Gifts

Loneliness can be an opportunity to deepen your relationship with yourself. It invites self-reflection, self-compassion, and self-discovery. Use this time to explore your inner world, to understand your needs and desires, and to cultivate a more profound connection with yourself.

Seeking Meaningful Social Connections

While solitude is valuable, it's equally essential to seek meaningful social connections when you're ready. Loneliness can be a signal that you need to connect with others. Reach out to friends, family, or support groups. Engaging in social activities that align with your interests can help you build new relationships.

Cultivating Quality Relationships

Quality trumps quantity when it comes to relationships. Focus on cultivating deep and meaningful connections with people who share your values and interests. These connections can provide genuine companionship and support during your journey of embracing solitude.

The Power of Vulnerability

Loneliness can be an opportunity to practice vulnerability. Share your feelings with trusted friends or a therapist. By opening up about our loneliness, we create space for understanding and empathy, allowing others to provide the support and connection we may need.

Engaging in Solo Activities

Learn to enjoy your own company by engaging in solo activities that bring you joy. Whether it's reading, hiking, painting, or simply savoring a cup of tea in silence, these moments of solitude can become cherished and fulfilling parts of your life.

Volunteering and Giving Back

Contributing to your community through volunteer work can be a powerful antidote to loneliness. It connects you with like-minded individuals and gives you a sense of purpose and fulfillment. Acts of kindness can also boost your own well-being.

Fostering Self-Compassion

Loneliness can lead to self-criticism and negative self-talk. Counter these tendencies, though, with what we discussed earlier, "self-compassion." Treat yourself kindly. Remember that you are not alone in experiencing the emotions.

Loneliness, like all emotions, comes and goes in waves. Some days you may feel its weight more acutely, while on others, it may recede into the background. Embrace this emotion, knowing that it is a temporary visitor on your journey of embracing solitude.

In the chapters ahead, we will explore how these experiences of loneliness can lead to greater self-awareness, personal growth, and an enhanced appreciation for the solitude you've chosen to embrace. Remember that loneliness is a teacher, guiding you toward a more profound connection with yourself and others as you continue along your path.

The Beauty of Solitude

Solitude, often feared or misunderstood, can be a profound source of growth and self-discovery. Embracing being alone is an opportunity to savor the freedom and tranquility that come with it.

Understanding Solitude
Solitude is not about isolation or loneliness but rather a deliberate choice to spend time with oneself. It provides a space for introspection, relaxation, and personal growth.

Cultivating Tranquility

Peace of Mind
Solitude provides a peaceful environment where you can attune to tranquil thoughts and feelings. In the absence of external noise and distractions, you can find inner calm.

Mindfulness and Relaxation
Practice mindfulness and relaxation techniques to fully embrace tranquility. Meditation, deep breathing exercises, and yoga can help you center your thoughts and be present in the moment.

The Joys of Savoring Moments Alone

Enjoying Simple Pleasures
Savoring solitude allows you to relish simple pleasures. Enjoy reading or writing a book, as I have done here, or taking a leisurely stroll, or savoring a quiet meal. These small moments of solitude can be incredibly fulfilling.

Nurturing Creativity and Inspiration

Creative Expression
Solitude provides an ideal environment for creative expression. Whether you're an artist, writer, or musician, alone time can be a wellspring of inspiration and innovation.

The Muse of Solitude
Many great thinkers and artists have found their most profound ideas and creations during moments of solitude. Embrace solitude as your muse, allowing ideas and insights to flow naturally.

Strengthening Emotional Resilience

Facing Emotions
Solitude encourages you to confront your emotions head-on. It's a safe space to experience and process feelings, whether they are joy, sadness, or contemplation. This emotional resilience can be empowering.

Fostering Independence and Self-Reliance

Self-Reliance Skills
Solitude is an opportunity to develop self-reliance skills. You become more adept at problem-solving and decision-making as you rely on your own judgment and resourcefulness.

Confidence Building
As you navigate life alone, your confidence grows. You learn to trust yourself and your abilities, which can positively impact all areas of your life.

Embracing Silence and Stillness

The Power of Silence
Silence is often underrated in a noisy world. Embracing silence allows you to hear your inner thoughts, find clarity, and experience deep peace. It's a valuable aspect of solitude.

Stillness and Mindful Presence
Practice stillness in your alone time. Sit quietly, observe your thoughts without judgment, and attune to the world around you. This mindful presence led me to a heightened sense of awareness.

The Balance of Social Connections and Solitude

While embracing solitude is essential, it's also crucial to strike a balance with social connections. Human interaction is a vital part of life, and it complements the tranquility and self-discovery found in solitude.

Building Meaningful Relationships
Embracing solitude can enhance your ability to form meaningful connections with others. When you have a strong sense of self and inner peace, the relationships you choose to be involved in are ones that tend to become more fulfilling and authentic.

The Art of Embracing Solitude

Embracing being alone, savoring freedom and solitude, and attuning to tranquil thoughts and feelings is an art that can transform your life. Solitude offered me the space to cultivate inner tranquility. It's a gift that, when embraced, can lead to a greater appreciation for the beauty of the present moment. Embrace solitude as a cherished part of your life's journey, and you'll find that it enriches your soul in ways you never imagined.

I recall resting my head on my pillow many times, and all I could focus on were my breathing and the crippling pains in my heart, and I cried out to God. Many tears fell one by one down my face. Suddenly, my pillow was totally soaked. I learned to hold my Bible close. I flipped through the Bible for comfort, and one verse I read many times was "How long must I wrestle with my thoughts and day after day have sorrow in my heart?" (Psalm 13:2).

I experienced much ongoing anxiety—spiritually, emotionally, mentally, and physically. Some days I would dwell on the sound of the birds and parrots in my tree in Miami, and other birds would be chirping in the sky, which was a beautiful blue, but I still would encounter those unexpected days in which everything suddenly seemed suffocating, and the idea of carrying on with my life seemed impossible. And there was not a "ten simple steps" program to get rid of that lonely anxiety. It was not easy to conquer.

So instead, here I offer you my experiences as someone who understands the battle through the process. Sometimes it's a struggle for the butterfly to emerge from the cocoon. The question I suggest is one that was constant in my mind: Is the struggle one that is necessary for the butterfly's full transformation and development? As I reflect on that profound question, it reminds me of the struggle in my cocoon phase while the butterfly was impatiently waiting to spread its wings.

God reminds us today, though, that He is preparing our wings during seasons of waiting and to put our trust in Him during the process. "And we know that all things work together for good, for those who love God, and are called according to his purpose" (Romans 8:28).

We can't always see where our future wings are going to take us, but God promises there's something better up ahead. We just need to trust Him.

Out of God's extreme sovereignty, He has completely freed me of much pain, anxiety, and worry. It is continuous healing. I can truly say I still feel the changes as they are happening within me. And when I began to feel mostly at peace, it was then I realized God is in extreme control of my life.

After leaving my first session at a Christian counseling center, I gained a better understanding of what exactly anxiety is and where it stems from in my personal life. My counselor said anxiety is "bottled-up emotions." All this time I had been containing my emotions, leaving me in a constant state of stress, fear, and worry.

That was a helpful step in the process, but it's also helpful to be reminded that the process continues, with more than "ten simple steps."

Depression is a dark, lonely place. For me, it felt as though I was trapped, drowning, with no hope of rescue. That was my reality for a long time. Depression must not be dismissed.

Real life doesn't afford staying in bed. In many moments, I felt profoundly broken. God, however, met me where I was, and He stuck with me.

When Abraham, childless and discouraged, sat in his tent, and cried, God showed up. Rather than reasoning with him, God offered Abraham hope as they walked and counted the stars (Genesis 15:1-6).

The problem with depression is that as the cells in our brain become unable to transmit or receive the right signals to regulate mood, our body may slow down; our stomach may tighten. We may lose our appetite or gain one. We may just want to sleep all the time, we may not be able to sleep, and on and on.

There is no quick fix, no simple solution, and acting like there is one is like throwing salt on the wound. Your situation is not the same as someone else's.

But that doesn't mean there is no help. The following are a few things I learned that were good for me. Maybe they will help you to navigate your own issues.

- Remember that you are not a mental health professional. Don't take authority, trying to fix yourself; approach your mental health with an open mind (if possible). Get professional help.
- Make no assumptions. As a friend of mine put it, "Depression is idiosyncratic; it's not a one-size-fits-all condition."
- You should try to have a professional present information while you listen.
- Assure trustworthy friends that you want them to hear what you are going through. We often hide, assuming our inner struggles will drive others away. Real friends are there for you—no matter what, the good or bad.
- Pray. Only God knows the full story.
- Embrace the complexity. Each situation is unique. What works for one individual may not work for another. Medication, exercise, diet, prayer, Scripture, meditating on Scripture, and healthy leisure are all proven ways to help, but overemphasizing the benefits of one to the exclusion of others can be problematic. Think holistically.

When a marriage takes a sharp left turn and ends in divorce, it can cause significant heartbreak, devastation, and loneliness for everyone involved. If this sounds similar to your own situation, don't lose hope. According to mental health experts and people who have experienced divorce, there are positive ways to cope with the loneliness and sadness caused by a breakup and heal your wounded heart.

When we marry, we hope our union will provide happiness, support, partnership, and love, and research shows most people feel optimistic about tying the knot. No wonder prolonged sadness after a divorce is not only common but expected, and comes with good reason, experts say.

It's important to remember that feelings of grief frequently felt leading up to, during, and after a divorce are very similar to what a person may feel after the death of a loved one.

How a Divorce Can Cause Grief

Experiencing sadness is common while navigating a divorce; for some people, these feelings may linger even years after the divorce is finalized. In fact, experiencing feelings of sadness anywhere from weeks to several years after the divorce is not unheard of.

Some of the more common reasons people feel sadness, also known as divorce grief, during and after a divorce include:

- Feeling rejected or abandoned
- Feeling insecure or uncertain about the future
- Loss of identity as a spouse
- The overall loss of a person and the partnership with that person
- Feelings of failure

This also explains why a person going through a divorce may be heartbroken even if they wanted the divorce. At the end of the day, loss is loss. And loss often comes with grief and sadness.

Don't rush the healing process. Allow yourself time to grieve, which will look different for each person. Keep in mind that this is a normal and healthy part of the process and give yourself time to heal.

There is sorrow that comes with letting go of the hope for the marriage to work and the dreams and goals you and your partner built over the years. There is also the impact your divorce has on your day-to-day life. Many times, a split means we are divorcing our partner's family and sometimes even mutual friend groups as well.

Having children involved can also raise the stakes in a divorce. There's confusion on how to properly communicate with them about what's happening and how best to comfort them while they're adjusting to the new normal, all the while tending to your own raw feelings. Guilt over how your divorce may affect your children can also deepen feelings of sadness and cause additional grief and stress.

Sometimes I felt guilty because I was unable to make the marriage work and feared that the children would suffer emotionally from the significant shift in the household. In many cases, this guilt only made the feelings that I already was experiencing worst.

Like sadness, feelings of loneliness come with the territory of divorce. Because many married couples build their lives around their partner, when a marriage dissolves, people are left feeling incomplete and yearning for the companionship they once had.

As was stated in *Psychology Today*, "Most married couples live very much enmeshed, which can make divorce all the more difficult, not only on a practical level in terms of splitting assets, custody, and so forth, but also in terms of being accustomed to having a thinking partner to problem-solve challenges with and bounce ideas off of." It is therefore understandable that the idea of not being married is terrifying to some people. I have spoken to many married couples who have stayed in unhappy marriages just because one or both did not want to go to bed alone at night.

That said, loneliness is a natural reaction to a divorce and a way to cope with the significant changes. Because many married couples spend a lot of time together and share so much of themselves, any significant change to that dynamic can cause emotional and mental trauma.

In fact, an article published in March 2023 in the International Journal of Environmental Research and Public Health found that loss of attachment and perceiving a lack of social support, as well as conflicts between ex-partners, can cause some divorced people to experience symptoms of post-traumatic stress disorder when having these thoughts. If you're having PTSD symptoms due to your marriage's end, speak with your doctor or a licensed therapist for mental health support.

How to Cope With Loneliness and Sadness After Divorce

Fortunately, there are active steps that you can take to cope with painful feelings during and immediately after a divorce. Speaking with a therapist who specializes in divorce can also help you better adjust to this big life transition.

> **1. Allow yourself time to mourn.** Allow yourself time to feel and to move past loneliness. Don't rush the healing process. Allow yourself time to grieve, which will look different for each person. Don't compare yourself with others. Keep in mind that this is a normal and healthy part of the process and give yourself time to heal.
>
> It's also not uncommon for divorced couples with shared custody to experience loneliness when their children are with the other parent. This may be especially true during the holidays. When this happens, I encourage you to remain kind to yourself and understand that it's natural to miss your children when they're with your ex-partner and to miss your former life. There will be good days and bad days.
>
> Healing after a divorce is not a linear process. We may have weeks when we feel great and then wake up one morning and run across a picture that triggers loneliness and sadness.
>
> **2. Stay positive.** While in grief, it may feel like the world is crashing down around you, but remember, it's possible to build a thriving and happy life after a divorce. Feelings of sadness and loneliness after a divorce should subside over time, and you will begin to find your footing again so that you're able to move on.
>
> Don't expect to wake up feeling completely intact overnight. Instead, anticipate a slow shift in your mood that gradually improves.
>
> **3. Practice self-love.** Remember, being kind to yourself during divorce is instrumental in getting through the most difficult times.

4. Focus on things that bring you joy. Being kind to yourself also includes intentional efforts to make time for self-care. The most important thing is that self-care brings you joy—for example, regular exercise, picking up a new or old hobby, or going out with friends.

Also important is setting boundaries and prioritizing your happiness in a healthy and productive way. Setting boundaries can be one of the best things a person can do as part of their self-care. Learn to say no to things that aren't in your best interest, and avoid engaging in triggering, negative, or upsetting conversations. Make sure that your family and friends respect those boundaries as well.

5. Don't do it all alone. If you are fortunate enough to have people in your life who you love and trust, ask them for support when you need it. Ask for a shoulder to cry on or for help with childcare or housing. Whatever you do, don't try to carry the weight of a divorce alone.

6. Take social media breaks. Social media can be a double-edged sword. Although social media can help people stay connected, numerous studies have found that it can also heighten feelings of loneliness.

It's easy to fall into a comparison trap on Facebook or Instagram, making your feelings of loneliness even more raw—like seeing your newly engaged coworker posting photos of their ring or your cousin's celebratory video about their fifteenth wedding anniversary. If you notice that social media is a negative trigger, step away from it for a bit to allow yourself time and space to heal.

7. Consider talking to a professional. Sorrow and loneliness are temporary in most cases, but sadness can spiral into depression. Seeking therapy is an additional form of support and is also an act of self-care regardless of whether you were the person who initiated the divorce. Even people who wanted a divorce can significantly benefit from speaking with a mental health professional.

Grief and Loneliness

If you're grieving, you may feel this has become the story of your life. There are aspects of grief that make loneliness seem inevitable and unsolvable—primarily the fact that what we desire is our loved one, and what we *have* is an emptiness molded so precisely to your loved one's likeness that no one else could ever fill it.

People who are grieving are at a disadvantage when it comes to loneliness because the person that they long for is gone. I've come to understand that loneliness after the loss of a loved one is many things. Above all else, it's the ache of having loved someone so much that pieces of you became them, and pieces of them became you. When they left, they took pieces of your shared life with them, and now you must live a life that feels incomplete. Some people may also say they lost one of the few people in the world who they thought truly "got" them.

Once your brain starts thinking in an "I'm on my own, so I have to look out for myself" kind of way, it may start to guard against others by pushing them away. And as you might expect, this perpetuates feelings of loneliness. You can't easily solve loneliness caused by grief. It takes time and effort. Instead, you must find other ways to connect and fill in alternative spaces, until healing arrives.

How do you do this? Sadly, I can't exactly answer that for you. However, I would say that when you are ready to open yourself to the love of new people in your life, then you will begin to slowly recognize new connections.

You can hold on to memories of your former loved one while at the same time accepting the company and support of others. And maybe, eventually, seeking out new people in the process, you will begin to discern a feeling. It won't be easy, and it won't be perfect, but in time, you can partially fill the void with another's love.

Comfort During Grief

Comfort is a natural desire that may be especially strong during times of pain and uncertainty. After experiencing a loss, you may find that comfort qualifies as a basic human need as it can help create a sense of security, safety, and stability in a world turned on its head.

No one would fault you for seeking heaps of comfort during grief any more than they would fault you for looking for water when lost in the desert. Though nothing can make right what feels very wrong, things like a hug from a friend, a piece of clothing that belonged to the person you lost, a comforting television show, or the security of home can connect you to those you love (both alive or dead) and provide a soothing and calm cocoon that drowns out the fear and unknown for a little while.

We can agree that comfort is generally good, and comfort during grief is essential. So, where's the catch?

Allowing Discomfort to Exist

While comfort is generally good, seeking it may sometimes be at odds with experiences that align with your wants, desires, values, and purpose. I often must remind myself that experiences aren't either/or—positive or negative, painful, or pleasant, comfortable, or uncomfortable.

When I was a kid, we swam in the ocean. It wasn't a chlorinated, heated pool. It was a COOL body of water, sometimes with seaweed and anything else we could imagine swimming below the dark surface. I loved swimming in the ocean, but getting in it was always a shock. So, my sister and I told ourselves if we just dove in and did a couple of bobs up and down, we'd get used to it. And you know what? We always got used to it after a while.

Many pleasant or positive experiences require us to push through a little discomfort. We may have to jump in, bob up and down, and remember that it won't take forever to get accustomed to the temperature or seaweed or whatever may feel strange. And if it stays uncomfortable, there's comfort to be found in uncomfortable situations as well. For example, the memory of your lost one. The ability to take a moment to yourself and breathe. Permission to leave an experience you hate. Or the simple knowledge that at the night's end, your comfy sofa will be at home waiting for you.

Grief Doesn't End; It Changes

The second matter we must agree on is that grief changes over time. If this weren't true, the idea that grief stays with us forever would mean a life of purgatory. Grief is always painful, but in the beginning, it is acute. It is a nightmare you may feel you can't wake up from as you are doubled over in agony, wondering *Does anything even matter?* Grief years later is far more manageable. You need to have faith that this is true.

The reality of grief is that it often stays with you until the day you, yourself, die to it. For those who think of grief as being an all-negative emotion, I can see where this may seem unmanageable, but rest assured the impact of grief changes over time.

As you change your relationship with grief, by changing how you respond to, cope with, and conceptualize it, you will likely also find hope and healing. If you think about it, grief is one instance where there is a strong benefit to accepting its ongoing presence in your life because doing so creates more room for comfort and positive memories.

Grief Years Later: Four Challenges

The first year of grief is nearly impossible. I've written about how, in some ways, the following years of grief can feel even harder. But what about after that? What about five years down the road or ten? Surely, there's nothing new to discover about your loss by that point.

It's not for me to predict how anyone will feel about their loss years down the line. Hundreds of different factors can influence the roads people take, the perspectives they find, and the things they make peace with. What I can say about grief years later is that many people continue to revisit and grapple with their loss experiences in different ongoing ways. I don't say any of this to scare you. I simply want anyone feeling surprised, frustrated, or dysfunctional because they're still mourning over their losses to know they are capital "N" normal.

People Stop Validating Your Loss

People often feel they can't bring up grief-related pain or seek support years after a loss. Most formal and informal support is offered in the weeks and months following the loss. Focusing a lot of attention here makes sense because so much is hard all at once. However, this, coupled with the misconception that grief ends, inadvertently can create a situation in which people feel silenced about their losses over time.

A person may feel that after a certain point, they shouldn't bring up their thoughts and feelings. They may fear people will think they're weak, seeking attention, or being dramatic. And indeed, many people have experiences that make them feel their grief over an older loss is less important or invalid.

Changing society's understanding of the ongoing nature of grief is a slow process. But in the meantime, if you want someone to speak to about your grief, it may be helpful to find a therapist or a supportive community that understands that grief has no time limit.

Continuing to Experience Secondary Losses

Secondary losses are losses that happen because of the primary loss. The primary loss is like a rock that's kicked up and puts a hole in your windshield. Secondary losses are all the cracks that splinter out from there.

When I talk to grieving people about secondary loss, I usually discuss secondary losses that become apparent immediately after the loss. But over time, I've realized through my own experiences that secondary losses are like an unwanted gift that keeps on giving.

As you go through life and have new experiences, you will likely stumble over additional secondary losses, some you never would have foreseen. For example, the loss of spending retirement with a spouse, the loss of having your parent become a grandmother, the loss of being able to call your spouse when things go wrong at work or with a friendship, etc. All these events can happen years after your initial loss, and because you continue to miss the person, you will likely feel their absence in new ways.

Connections Sever and Losses Accumulate
As people grow older, they accumulate loss; they move away from places, get new jobs, lose touch with friends, and people die. Ideally, you carry the people and places you cherish forward with you. However, it still hurts to lose tangible connections to the past.

These things may have grounded you and reminded you where you came from. Or perhaps they connected you to people who are gone. Regardless, additional loss and change, along with time passing, leave people with the sense that the life they lived with people in the past is getting further and further away. And that sometimes makes individuals feel sad.

Memories Become More Abstract
Most of us who are grieving, or have grieved, already know one of the saddest things about life after loss is that, with time, memories like the sound of a loved one's voice, the smell of their perfume, their clothes, or the feeling of their arms wrapped around you start to fade.

Sensory memories are tied closely to a person's physical presence, and, in the beginning, there's nothing you want more. Arguably, the loss of these sensory experiences is one of the first secondary losses a person will experience after a death. Sensory memories are short; technically, we can only hold onto sounds and smells for approximately half of a second. This is why many people hold onto things like old clothes, voicemails, cards with their loved one's handwriting, photographs, cologne, etc. These things help to trigger those sensory memories. But, with time, even those things will mostly fade or become lost. The older we get, the more difficult it is to hold onto sharp, detailed memories. Luckily, some people have excellent memories.

However, if you're like me, you may find that specific memories grow more abstract over time. They become ideas, stories, and words, but the pictures and feelings they once evoked are difficult to grasp.

Loneliness after a divorce or breakup is common and even expected. You were sharing a life with your spouse or partner, maybe raising kids, and likely making plans for a future together. Divorce and breakups stir up strong emotions, many of which can lead to feelings of loneliness.

What are the causes and what can you do to help manage loneliness after a divorce?

What Causes You to Feel Lonely After a Divorce or Breakup?

When a relationship ends, there are several factors that can contribute to post-breakup loneliness:

- o Grief, sadness, and anger: Divorce and relationship breakups can start you on an emotional roller coaster. Grief, sadness, and even anger can be common. Emotions like these may cause you to pull away from others and isolate yourself, which can eventually lead to feelings of loneliness.

- o Separation from family and friends: When divorce and breakups happen, it's not uncommon to become separated from groups of friends and extended family, especially those closest to your ex. These people were an important part of your shared life and could very well be completely gone from your new life. And let's not forget about pets. Many divorces and breakups also mean a beloved family pet is going with one partner and not the other.

- Child custody: When children are involved in a divorce, there are often custody issues to deal with. If you share custody with an ex, there could be times you suddenly find yourself alone without kids around to distract you. This can contribute to feelings of loneliness after divorce also.
- Holiday blues: Many couples and families have regular holiday traditions, often shared with family and friends. Divorce and breakups can change all that. When those holidays come back around, they may bring with them post-relationship loneliness.

What Are Some Ways to Deal with Loneliness After a Relationship Ends?

Consider these tips:

- Accept your feelings of post-relationship loneliness: You've suddenly lost someone important in your life. They are physically gone, as well as emotionally. You may feel disconnected and alienated from others as well. While you grieve and heal your split, you may experience periods of loneliness that can be a common part of the process in moving forward.
- Avoid a rebound relationship: Don't let loneliness after your breakup or divorce push you to dive into relationships trying to find yourself. If you're using a rebound relationship to avoid loneliness or the emotions of a breakup, you may want to reconsider. Instead, try spending some healing time with yourself before embarking again on the dating path.
- Join a support group for divorced people: You're not alone. Therapy groups offer an opportunity to get help, understanding, and insight from others who are going through a similar experience. Loneliness after divorce is quite common, and chances are good you will discover others in your situation who are willing to talk, listen, and offer advice.

- Start a new routine: Losing a relationship can also mean your way of life has drastically changed. If you lived with your spouse or partner, it's likely you had a regular, everyday routine. The longer the relationship or marriage, the more ingrained that day-to-day routine became. A split can suddenly upend all of that, leaving you feeling disoriented and directionless. Things like mealtimes, sleep schedules, and even exercise regimens can fall by the wayside, impacting your health and wellness. If you exercised regularly, then get back to it. Exercise alone can help boost endorphins, which can make you feel happier. So, try planning out a new routine for yourself. See if it can help offset some of the factors contributing to any post-breakup loneliness you may be feeling.

- Get involved: Volunteering or joining a club, engaging with other people, can help boost your mood and make you a happier person. Look for volunteer options with likeminded people. Be open to building lasting friendships and a new support network.

- Remember again, be good to yourself: Find special things that delight just you. Try to carve out a few enjoyable moments every day. Maybe you'd enjoy a walk or hike, a bubble bath, some yoga, reading a good book, or listening to your favorite music. Whatever it is that brings you immediate enjoyment, spend the time doing it. Building good habits like this can help you fight feeling lonely when your relationship ends.

How Long Do Feelings of Loneliness After a Breakup or Divorce Last?

Feelings of social isolation and disengagement from others may not be constant—they may be driven by a particular situation or may come and go. For example, a holiday that rolls back around may bring with it a period of loneliness that fades after the holiday.

For most people, loneliness that occurs after a divorce or breakup is temporary and part of the grieving and healing process. If loneliness goes on and on and seems never-ending, it may be time to talk to your doctor, a therapist, or another health care provider about chronic loneliness as they will be able to help.

Loneliness sucks. It's a horrible feeling to think you have nobody in the world. Like all these emotions we are dealing with, mindful strategies exist that you can use to help you start feeling better, even when you think you cannot be consoled.

Let's look here!

Being alone after divorce **does not mean being lonely.**

When we are by ourselves after divorce, we make a false correlation in our minds. We think that being alone is negative and bad for us. We can't stand the silence, we feel weird sleeping in a bed alone, and we feel uneasy saying "I" instead of "we."

When you feel lonely after divorce, ask yourself, why is being alone a bad thing?

It's not.

If you want to stop feeling lonely after divorce, you can breathe. You have the opportunity to heal and start over on your terms. These things could have been impossible if you were still with someone who wasn't giving you the love and respect you deserve, even the needed space to grow.

When you are lonely after divorce, remember that even when you were with someone in an unhealthy relationship, you might have still been lonely. Do you remember all the times when you felt the sadness and silence when you were married?

Living with a partner in a marriage that is no longer healthy and still feeling alone is much more damaging than being by yourself in a house and having the space to heal on your own terms. I remember coming home from work and driving past the house a couple of times before pulling in the driveway. I was with someone, but yet alone.

See the difference?

Loneliness After Divorce Is Independence and Liberation Waiting for a Spark of Hope

Many of us tend to view loneliness as a solitary confinement that we can't break free from. But I'm here to tell you that you don't have time for that!

To stop feeling lonely after divorce, there are barriers to overcome. Yes, you may feel like there is nobody to call or to be intimate with. When you heal, you may become self-conscious with friends because you don't want to be a burden. Feeling like you can't reach out even though you feel awful only doubles that terrible feeling.

If you want to stop feeling lonely after divorce, turn that sense of being by yourself into something new.

Sure, you do not have people around you, but doesn't that give you the opportunity to start doing things you never thought you could do before? Instead of staying at home, you now have an opportunity to channel that energy into attending a class, joining a book club, planning a trip. There is nobody to stop you or judge you, and you can now do the things you've wanted to do for the longest time. Take advantage of all of it!

Stop Feeling Lonely after Divorce Exercise 1: The Love Mindset

If you are unsure where to start, I have included some of the ways I used to help keep the Loneliness Monster at bay. You will see that whenever we show ourselves kindness and are proactive about taking back our lives, we are embracing the Love Mindset.

Ask yourself: When do I feel lonely? Are there certain events that trigger those emotions for me?

Do not spend too much time on this part of the exercise. The point is to merely acknowledge your triggers so you can move on to the Love Mindset.

Maybe you get triggered whenever friends post photos of their engagement rings on Facebook, reminding you that now you have no one. Or you feel lonely whenever you see a little old couple holding hands and walking in the park.

Now comes the fun part...

Ask yourself: Who am I when I am the happiest? When am I at my best?

The Love Mindset: I feel happy when I am around my grandchildren. There is a soft spot in my heart for them.

The Love Mindset: I feel that the true me comes out when I am travelling and exploring new things. I become a curious, happier person when I am exploring a museum with nobody there to distract me or wandering through a new shop in a new neighborhood in a new city, where anything is possible.

The Love Mindset: All my worries seem to disappear when I am working hard in a class. I love how it makes me feel and how it forces me to focus and listen and communicate. At the end of the class, I always feel relieved and ready to take on the world.

Discovering what brings out the best in you and what makes you happy doesn't have to cost money. It does, however, mean that you will have to be introspective and honest with yourself. It can be hard to dig deep, but I promise you that it is worth it, because you are feeling better, and being happy is worth it.

Now that you know what triggers your loneliness and what makes you feel happy and the best version of yourself, we need to bridge that gap with the final step.

Ask Yourself: What can I do right now to summon that amazing part of me? That part that will help me through those periods of loneliness?

The Love Mindset: The next time I see a Facebook picture of an engagement ring, I am going to shut that page off instead. My time and energy are better served helping those in need, and who on earth can feel lonely while they are taking care of the parts of the Kingdom that needs developing, people who need food, a good home, clothing, etc.?

The Love Mindset: The house feels so empty, and I am starting to feel alone. But I remember there's that new African American Museum in DC that I can visit or a new movie out that I want to see. Why don't I check the hours and go?

See how that exercise works?

Recognize that you deserve to be happy and understand that spending quality time by yourself and in a life that is rich with ideas and hobbies and things that excite and inspire you—and have absolutely nothing to do with having a partner—can be what is needed to heal you.

Being open to all the wonderful things this world can offer, and fully acknowledging that you are in this world to explore it, to dominate it, help it, is the antidote to loneliness. When you begin the love story with yourself, you always have someone at your side.

Loneliness is a prevalent and global problem for adult populations, and several different studies have linked it to multiple chronic conditions, including heart disease, lung disease, cardiovascular disease, hypertension, atherosclerosis, stroke, and metabolic disorders, such as obesity and metabolic disease. It is a major predictor of psychological problems such as depression, psychological stress, and anxiety.

Loneliness is linked to overall morbidity and mortality in adult populations. But limited interventions have demonstrated long-term effectiveness in reducing loneliness in adults with these same chronic conditions.

Loneliness Is a Multidimensional and Complex Construct

Loneliness and isolation are two different issues: a person can be alone and not feel alone and vice versa.

Psychologists affirm that loneliness is a natural phenomenon, a personal feeling that may arise at certain moments in life and affect anyone, regardless of gender, age, or other socio-demographic characteristics. They also explain that loneliness is often seen as rooted in weakness or self-pity, as something that supposedly the individual should be able to eliminate, since it is not a physical ailment. Furthermore, they make the distinction between emotional loneliness and social loneliness. Other authors have defined loneliness from different perspectives: as a negative psychological response to a discrepancy between the social relationships one desires (expectations) and the relationships one actually has (objective, real ones); as an individual feeling characterized by an unpleasant or inadmissible lack of quality in certain social relationships that can occur either because one has fewer social contacts than one wishes to have, or because the level of intimacy hoped for in relationships is not there; as the subjective component of the objective measure of social isolation; in other words, loneliness would be the inverse of a situation of social support; as a social pain, something comparable to physical pain, because if physical pain arises to protect us from physical dangers, loneliness would manifest itself as a way to protect us from the danger of remaining isolated, related to the importance of social connections.

In general, it is assumed that emotional loneliness refers to the absence of an attachment figure, together with feelings of isolation, and social loneliness as the lack of a social network, the absence of a circle of people that allows an individual to develop a sense of belonging, of company, of being part of a community.

Both in daily life and in the research area, various researchers have referred to "loneliness" and "social isolation" indistinctly. Others, however, find both terms very different from each other.

Making accurate evaluations depends on a clear definition of the concept of loneliness, with special awareness of its multidimensionality and its differences with respect to related concepts (social isolations or a lack of social support). Loneliness and isolation place people at risk of vulnerability or social frailty; this dynamic concept of scarcity is closely linked to sustainability, development, social exclusion, poverty, and the lack of social support resources. Furthermore, social vulnerability is closely tied to physical frailty and mortality.

However, you look at it, loneliness, that sense of lacking or privation, exerts a powerful influence over our health. There are multiple facets to loneliness: there are feelings of emptiness or abandonment associated with a lack of relationships or intimacy; there is the temporal perspective (loneliness sets in over time) through which the individual perceives his or her own loneliness; there is the set of emotional aspects that accompany loneliness, including sadness, melancholy, frustration, shame or desperation; and, there is the individual's own subjective evaluation regarding the quality and quantity of his or her social relationships, built and rebuilt by the people in their lives, an evaluation which depends on the continuous interaction between factors which are rather diverse (identity, personality, expectations, life events, interpersonal engagement, socio-economic variables, household, etc.). Yet, despite all of this, while effective interventions are necessary, they may be scarce.

Social isolation is an objective and quantifiable reflection of the reduction in the size of the social network and the lack of social contact, but Isaiah 26:4 includes the metaphor of a rock, which depicts the security and safety found in God: "The Lord, the Lord himself, is the Rock eternal." Figuratively, what's described is a refuge. This word is used three times in Psalm 18 (vv. 2, 31, 46). In verse 2, the psalmist multiplies metaphors to stress divine dependability: "The Lord is my rock, my fortress and my deliverer; my God is my rock, in whom I take refuge, my shield and the horn of my salvation, my stronghold."

In Isaiah 26:4 the word means long duration, forever, everlasting, perpetual: "The Lord, the Lord himself, is the Rock eternal." The pairing of these words enhances God's credibility exponentially. Trust Him. His faithfulness is unending!

My friend, you are not alone. There is hope. You have a purpose, and the Lord himself is there to help you.

*In the midst of solitude,
you find the company of your own strength.*

Reflect & Pray

Father, I know I get caught up in the fast pace of life. Help me to make room for You in everything I do.

> **Why we must trust the process:**
> 1. God's plan is perfect (Jeremiah 29:11)
> 2. To overcome fear and anxiety (Philippians 4:6-7)
> 3. To strengthen our faith (Hebrews 11:6)
> 4. It leads to blessings and growth (James 1:2-4)
>
> — Pastor Ken
>
> **TRUST THE PROCESS**

Chapter 6

DATING AGAIN: A NEW ADVENTURE

After navigating the depths of solitude and embracing the power of self-love, you may at some point consider the prospect of dating again. This chapter explores the complexities and opportunities of reentering the dating world after "singleness."

The Decision to Date

Deciding to date again is a highly personal choice, and there's no right or wrong time to begin. It's essential to examine your motivations. Are you seeking companionship, validation, or a genuine connection? Ensure your reasons align with your values and personal growth goals.

Self-Exploration Continues

Before stepping into the dating scene, take time for self-reflection. Have you learned from past relationships? Do you have a clear sense of your values, boundaries, and what you're looking for in a partner? This self-exploration is crucial for healthy dating.

Setting Healthy Expectations

Dating can be exciting, but it can also bring expectations and potential disappointments. Set realistic expectations for yourself and your potential partners. Understand that no one is perfect, and dating is a process of getting to know someone.

Online Dating and Apps

Online dating has become a common way to meet new people.

If you choose to use dating apps or websites, approach them with caution. Be selective about the platforms you use and prioritize safety. Remember that online profiles provide only a glimpse of a person's life.

Honesty and Authenticity

Authenticity is key in dating. Be yourself and communicate your intentions clearly. Honesty fosters trust and helps you find compatible partners who appreciate you for who you are.

Navigating Rejection

Rejection is an inherent part of dating, and it can be painful. Remember that rejection doesn't reflect your worth or desirability as a person. It's merely an indication of incompatibility. Use rejection as an opportunity to practice resilience and self-compassion.

Building Healthy Connections

Focus on building healthy connections based on shared values, interests, and mutual respect. Take your time to get to know potential partners and assess whether they align with your long-term goals.

Red Flags and Boundaries

Pay attention to red flags in potential relationships. If something doesn't feel right, trust your instincts, and set boundaries. Your well-being and safety should always come first.

Embracing Independence

Dating should complement your life, not define it. Maintain your independence and continue to prioritize self-care, personal goals, and friendships outside of romantic relationships.

Timing and Patience

Timing matters in dating. Don't rush into a new relationship if you're not ready. Be patient and allow connections to develop naturally. Remember that the journey of embracing solitude is about self-discovery, and dating should enhance your life, not complete it.

In the chapters ahead, we will explore the dynamics of forming healthy relationships and maintaining your independence while dating. Whether you choose to embrace the single life or pursue a romantic partnership, know that your journey is uniquely yours, and every experience contributes to your growth and self-discovery.

Exploration of healthy personal decisions when it comes to DATING AGAIN, including considerations about potential partners, boundaries, cautiousness, and patience:

The Decision to Date Again

Deciding to date again after a period of being single or after a previous relationship is a significant personal choice. This journey requires careful consideration of your own needs, values, and desires.

Self-Reflection
Before diving into the dating world, take time for self-reflection. Understand what you're looking for in a partner and what you bring to a relationship. This self-awareness will guide your choices.

Setting Healthy Relationship Goals

Clearly define your relationship goals. Are you seeking a casual dating experience, a committed partnership, or something else entirely? Your goals will help you make decisions that align with your desires.

Prioritizing Compatibility
When considering potential partners, prioritize compatibility. Look for individuals who share your values, interests, and long-term vision for a relationship. This sets a strong foundation for a healthy connection.

Establishing Personal Boundaries

Understanding Boundaries
Boundaries are essential in any relationship. Before dating again, establish your personal boundaries, what you're comfortable with and what you're not. Communicate these boundaries clearly.

Respecting Your Own Limits
It's crucial to respect your own boundaries and to expect the same from potential partners. Boundaries help maintain emotional and physical well-being in a relationship.

Exercising Caution

Cautiousness is about approaching dating with care and mindfulness. Take your time to get to know potential partners, and don't rush into decisions. Your safety and emotional well-being matter.

Pay attention to red flags and assess the trustworthiness of potential partners. Trust should be earned over time, not given blindly.

Patience in the Dating Process

Patience is a virtue when it comes to dating. Understand that finding the right partner may take time, and that's okay. Rushing into a relationship can lead to unfulfilling connections.

Avoiding Settling
Resist the urge to settle for a relationship that doesn't align with your goals, visions, or values. Patience allows you to hold out for a partnership that truly enriches your life.

The Role of Communication

Communication is the cornerstone of any healthy relationship. Be open and honest with potential partners about your intentions, expectations, and boundaries. Encourage them to do the same.

Active Listening
Active listening is equally important. Pay attention to what your potential partner communicates verbally and nonverbally. It helps build mutual understanding.

Building Emotional Resilience

Understanding Rejection
Remember what I said in the beginning of this chapter? Rejection is a part of dating. It's essential to understand that rejection isn't a reflection of your worth. Building emotional resilience will help you bounce back from setbacks.

Self-Compassion
Practice self-compassion during challenging moments in the dating process. Be kind to yourself and avoid self-blame. Remember that dating is also a journey with both highs and lows.

Healthy Relationship Dynamics

Balancing Independence and Togetherness
Healthy relationships strike a balance between independence and togetherness. It's essential to maintain your individuality while fostering a meaningful connection.

Addressing Conflict Constructively
Conflict is natural in any relationship. Learn how to address conflicts constructively, focusing on resolution and growth rather than argument and blame.

Trusting Your Instincts

Trusting Your Gut
Your instincts can be a valuable guide in dating. If something feels off or uncomfortable, trust your gut. It's okay to walk away from situations that don't align with your well-being.

Continuous Self-Reflection
Continue to reflect on your dating experiences and adjust your approach as needed. Trusting your instincts is an ongoing process.

Navigating the world of dating involves a series of healthy personal decisions. By setting clear goals, establishing boundaries, exercising caution, and practicing patience, you can approach dating with confidence and authenticity. Remember that each dating experience is an opportunity for personal growth and self-discovery. Embrace the journey with an open heart and a commitment to building meaningful, fulfilling friendships.

"The beauty of life lies in its unpredictability; embrace the unknown." — Yorthee Forger

Reflect & Pray

Father, I praise You for bringing my brokenness back together again. Thank you, Father, for working to bring our fractured world together.

"And we know that all things work together for good to them that love God and are called according to his purpose" (Romans 8:28).

> **Trusting the process is trusting the isolation.**
> — Pastor Karen
>
> TRUST THE PROCESS

Chapter 7

OVERCOMING RELATIONSHIP BAGGAGE

Embracing solitude often involves a journey of healing and self-discovery, and one crucial aspect of this journey is addressing and overcoming the baggage from past relationships. In this chapter, we'll explore how to untangle the emotional threads of your past and build a healthier foundation for the future.

The Weight of Baggage

Relationship baggage refers to the emotional scars, unresolved issues, and negative patterns carried forward from previous relationships. It can manifest as trust issues, fear of vulnerability, or lingering pain from past heartbreaks. Recognizing and addressing this baggage is essential for personal growth.

Reflecting on Past Relationships

Begin by reflecting on your past relationships, both the good and the challenging.

What patterns or recurring issues do you notice? What have you learned about yourself and your needs? Understanding the dynamics of your past can shed light on your relationship baggage.

Forgiving and Letting Go

One of the most powerful steps in overcoming relationship baggage is forgiveness. This includes forgiving your former partner(s) for any hurts or disappointments and forgiving yourself for any mistakes or regrets. Forgiveness liberates you from carrying the weight of resentment and allows you to move forward.

Closure can be an important part of healing from past relationships. If there are unresolved issues or unanswered questions, consider seeking closure through communication or self-reflection. Sometimes, closure is not about receiving answers from others but finding them within yourself.

Recognizing and Challenging Patterns

Identify any negative patterns that have emerged in your relationships. Do you tend to repeat the same mistakes or attract similar partners? Recognizing these patterns is the first step in breaking free from them. Challenge yourself to make different choices moving forward.

Healing from relationship baggage requires self-compassion. Understand that it's normal to carry scars from past experiences, but those scars don't define you. Treat yourself with kindness as you navigate the healing process.

Seeking Professional Support

Therapy or counseling can be immensely beneficial in addressing relationship baggage. A trained therapist can help you explore your emotions, provide tools for healing, and guide you in developing healthier relationship patterns.

Overcoming relationship baggage often involves a willingness to be vulnerable. Embrace vulnerability as a strength rather than a weakness. Opening yourself to the possibility of hurt is also opening up to the possibility of love and connection.

Setting Healthy Boundaries

Healthy boundaries are crucial in preventing the recurrence of past relationship issues. Establish clear boundaries in your future relationships and communicate them openly with your partner. Boundaries protect your emotional well-being.

The Path to Freedom

Overcoming relationship baggage is a transformative journey toward emotional freedom. It allows you to enter new relationships with a lighter, softer heart and a deeper understanding of yourself. It's an affirmation that your past does not define your future.

In the chapters ahead, we will explore how addressing and overcoming relationship baggage can lead to healthier, more fulfilling relationships or deepen your appreciation for the solitude you've chosen to embrace. Remember that your past is a part of your story, but it does not have to dictate your future.

Let's explore the art of letting go of unhealthy past relationships and avoiding desperate rebounds:

Overcoming Relationship Baggage, the Weight of Unhealthy Baggage

The art of letting go and avoiding desperate rebounds is essential for reclaiming emotional well-being and finding healthier connections.

Recognizing Unhealthy Baggage
The first step in this journey is recognizing the unhealthy baggage you carry. This may include unresolved emotions, lingering attachments, and negative patterns of thinking and behavior stemming from past relationships.

The Healing Process

Embracing the Healing Journey
Healing from an unhealthy past relationship is a process that requires time and self-compassion. Understand that it's okay to grieve the loss, experience pain, and confront difficult emotions. This is an essential part of the healing journey.

Seeking Support
Remember, as stated in previous chapters, don't hesitate to seek support from friends, family, or a therapist. Talking about your experiences and feelings can be therapeutic and provide valuable perspectives on the healing process.

Self-Reflection and Personal Growth

Understanding Patterns
Take time for self-reflection to understand the patterns that led to the unhealthy relationship. Identify the red flags and behaviors that you want to avoid in future connections.

Committing to Personal Growth
The healing process is an opportunity for personal growth. Commit to self-improvement, whether it's through self-help books, therapy, or personal development workshops. Focus on becoming the best version of yourself.

The Art of Letting Go

Embracing the Power of Letting Go
Letting go is a transformative art. It involves releasing attachments, forgiving both yourself and your past partner, and making room for new opportunities and positive emotions.

Forgiving Yourself and Others
Forgiveness is a significant part of letting go. Forgive yourself for any mistakes or regrets and extend forgiveness to your past partner. This is a powerful step toward emotional freedom.

Avoiding Desperate Rebounds

Understanding Rebound Relationships
Rebound relationships often occur when individuals rush into new connections to fill the void left by an unhealthy past relationship. These relationships are often based on desperation rather than genuine compatibility.

Taking a Break from Dating
Consider taking a break from dating to focus on self-healing and personal growth. Rushing into a new relationship can hinder your emotional recovery and lead to repeating unhealthy patterns.

Building Emotional Resilience

Emotional Resilience and Self-Love
Building emotional resilience is essential to avoid desperate rebounds. Cultivate self-love, self-compassion, and self-worth. These qualities will empower you to make healthy choices in relationships.

Loneliness is a common challenge after letting go of an unhealthy relationship. Instead of rushing into a rebound, embrace your alone time as an opportunity for self-discovery and self-nurturing.

Setting Healthy Relationship Goals

Clarifying Relationship Goals
Before considering a new relationship, clarify your relationship goals.
What are you seeking in a partner?
What qualities and values are essential to you?
Setting clear goals will guide your choices.

The Importance of Communication

Open and Honest Communication
Communication is vital in any healthy relationship. Be open and honest with your potential partner about your intentions, expectations, and boundaries. Encourage them to do the same.

Building Trust Gradually
Trust should be built gradually in a new relationship. Take your time to get to know your partner, and don't rush into vulnerability. Trust is an essential foundation for a healthy connection.

Embracing Independence and Self-Reliance

Balancing Independence and Togetherness
Healthy relationships strike a balance between independence and togetherness. Maintain your individuality while fostering a meaningful connection.

Strengthening Self-Reliance

Develop self-reliance skills. This involves making decisions independently, pursuing your passions, and prioritizing self-care. Self-reliance enhances your well-being and adds value to any relationship.

The Art of Emotional Liberation

Letting go of past unhealthy relationships and avoiding desperate rebounds is an art that leads to emotional liberation and healthier connections. It involves healing, self-reflection, forgiveness, and the courage to embrace personal growth. Remember that the journey to healthier relationships begins with self-love and a commitment to making choices that align with your well-being. By practicing these principles, you can cultivate lasting happiness and find relationships that truly enrich you.

As you may be realizing, I indulged in my fair share of self-help books over the years, ranging from detailed accounts of self-esteem issues, depression, tips and tricks for beating loneliness; the stories offered only a few moments of fleeting comfort as I moved through the pages, but they could not take the sting out of the emotions I was feeling firsthand.

Therefore, I had to learn to take only the advice that worked best for my own situation and leave the rest for someone else. Sometimes I just had to give myself a break to rest and restore. Go at your own pace, my friend, and only you will know when it feels right to take a brave step out of your comfort zone and into the unknown. It's okay to feel lonely; it is a human emotion. Try to enjoy the detachment.

Remember your past because it is what brought you to this point in time and embrace your future with gratefulness for the new that is coming and will be brought to you. And then get excited about the joy, love, and peace you have to look forward to.

*We are not defined by our past;
we are being prepared for our future.*

Reflect & Pray

Father, thank You for allowing me to see my new life in You. The old has gone, and the new is here!

"Therefore, if any man be in Christ, he is a new creature: old things are passed away, behold all things are become new" (2 Corinthians 5:17).

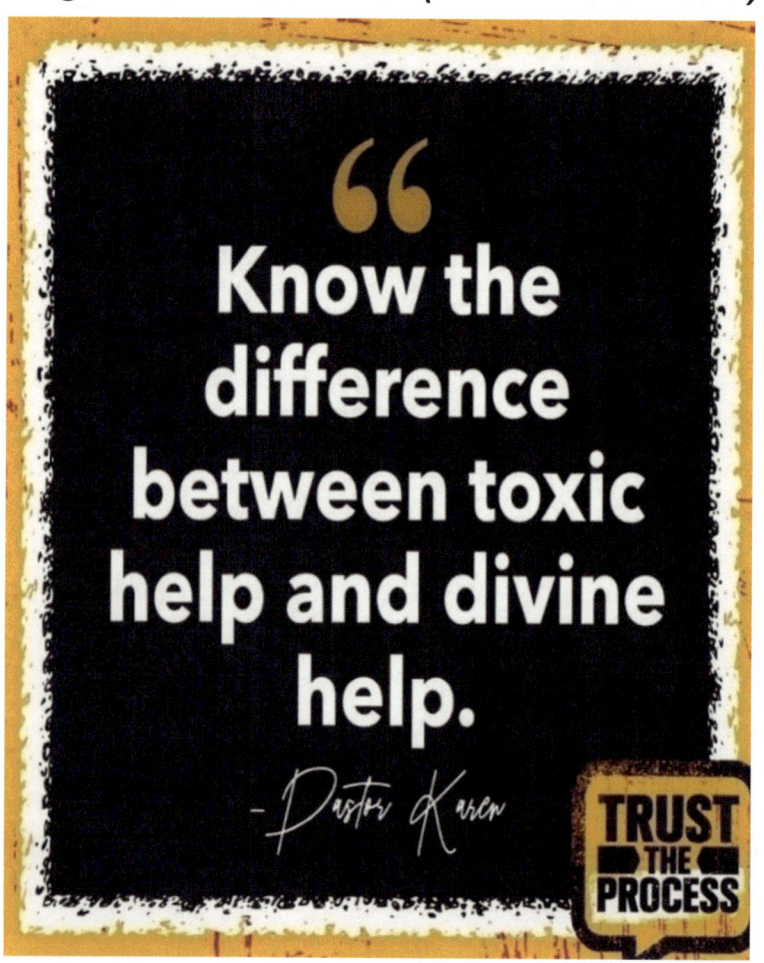

> Know the difference between toxic help and divine help.
> — Pastor Karen

TRUST THE PROCESS

Chapter 8

BALANCING INDEPENDENCE AND PARTNERSHIP

As we embrace solitude and possibly explore new relationships, finding the delicate balance between independence and partnership becomes a vital aspect of our journey. In this chapter, we'll explore how to maintain our autonomy while fostering healthy connections with others.

Autonomy as a Foundation

Autonomy is the cornerstone of a healthy and balanced life. It's the capacity to make independent choices, set personal goals, and lead a life that aligns with your values. As you navigate the path of embracing solitude, remember that your independence is an essential part of who you are.

The Allure of Independence

Independence offers a sense of freedom and self-reliance. It allows you to prioritize your own needs, make decisions that align with your goals, and build a life that reflects your authentic self. Cherish the allure of independence and recognize its inherent value.

Building a Healthy Partnership

Healthy partnerships are built on mutual respect, shared values, and open communication. When entering a new relationship, ensure that it complements your independence rather than detracts from it. Choose a partner who appreciates your autonomy and encourages your personal growth.

Communication Is Key

Effective communication is the essence of balancing independence and partnership. Discuss your needs, boundaries, and goals with your partner openly and honestly. Encourage your partner to do the same. This transparency fosters understanding and helps maintain a healthy balance.

Setting and Respecting Boundaries

Boundaries play a pivotal role in balancing independence and partnership. Clearly define your boundaries and communicate them to your partner. Respect your partner's boundaries as well. Healthy boundaries protect your autonomy while nurturing the relationship.

Quality Time vs. Alone Time

Finding the right balance between spending quality time with your partner and preserving your alone time can be challenging. It's essential to strike a harmonious equilibrium that allows for connection while honoring your need for solitude.

Pursuing Shared Interests

Engaging in shared interests or hobbies can be a wonderful way to bond with your partner while maintaining independence. It allows you to spend time together without sacrificing your individuality.

Personal Growth in Partnership

Healthy partnerships can be catalysts for personal growth. Encourage each other to pursue individual passions, set personal goals, and evolve as individuals. Your personal growth should complement and enrich your partnership.

Navigating Challenges Together

Every relationship encounters challenges. Remember that facing difficulties together is an opportunity for growth and strengthening your bond. Maintain open lines of communication and collaborate on solutions that respect both your independence and your partnership.

Celebrating Interdependence

The goal is to achieve a state of interdependence—a relationship where both partners maintain their independence while relying on each other for emotional support and connection. Interdependence celebrates the synergy of two unique individuals coming together.

In the chapters ahead, we will explore how balancing independence and partnership can lead to a fulfilling and harmonious life, whether you choose to remain single or embrace a new relationship. Your journey is about finding your unique balance and continuing to grow both as an independent individual and as a partner in a healthy, loving connection.

The Importance of Balance in Relationships

Balancing partnership and independence is a fundamental aspect of healthy and fulfilling relationships. Achieving this equilibrium allows individuals to nurture their individuality while building strong, committed bonds with their partners.

Understanding the Struggle
Many people face challenges in maintaining balance within relationships. This struggle often stems from societal expectations, personal insecurities, or past experiences. Finding the right balance requires self-awareness and communication.

Nurturing Individuality

Embracing Personal Passions
Individuality thrives when personal passions are nurtured. Encourage each other to pursue hobbies and interests

independently, allowing both partners to grow and find joy outside the relationship.

Independence and Identity
Maintaining independence is vital for preserving one's identity within a partnership. Each person should have a sense of self that extends beyond the relationship. This self-identity strengthens the bond between partners.

Clear Communication

Open and Honest Communication
I can't say this enough: effective communication is the cornerstone of finding balance. Partners should openly discuss their needs, desires, and boundaries. It's crucial to create a safe space where both individuals can express themselves freely.

Expressing Individual Needs
Encourage your partner to express their individual needs and desires. This fosters understanding and helps avoid assumptions or unmet expectations.

Setting Boundaries

Defining Personal Space
Again, setting boundaries is essential for maintaining independence. Clearly define personal space and time that each partner can use for themselves, free from intrusion or expectations.

Respecting Boundaries
Respecting these boundaries is equally important. It demonstrates trust, understanding, and a commitment to each other's well-being.

Mutual Support and Encouragement

Partners should be each other's biggest cheerleaders. Encourage and support your partner's goals and dreams, whether they are career-oriented or personal. This support helps you thrive and grow.

Celebrate Individual Achievements
Celebrate each other's individual achievements. These milestones are a testament to personal growth and should be cherished within the relationship.

Quality Time Together

While maintaining independence, it's also essential to balance togetherness. Quality time spent together strengthens the emotional bond and creates shared memories.

Establish relationship rituals or traditions that allow partners to connect and bond. These can be weekly dates, annual vacations, or even simple routines.

Solving Conflicts Gracefully

Conflict Resolution
Conflict is a natural part of any relationship. When conflicts arise, address them gracefully. Focus on resolving the issue rather than attacking each other's independence.

Seeking Compromise
Finding a compromise that respects both partners' needs is key. Effective conflict resolution strengthens the relationship and maintains the balance between partnership and independence.

The Importance of Trust

Trust is the foundation of a healthy partnership. Building and maintaining trust allow both individuals to feel secure in their independence and the relationship.

Jealousy can be a threat to independence and trust. Address any feelings of jealousy openly, and work together to overcome them.

Reevaluating and Adjusting

The Changing Nature of Balance
Finding balance in partnership and independence is not a static achievement. It evolves as individuals and relationships grow and change. Periodically reevaluate the balance to ensure it aligns with current needs and desires.

Adjusting as Necessary
Be willing to adjust and adapt. Life circumstances, personal goals, and external factors can influence the balance within a relationship. Flexibility is key to maintaining harmony.

The Art of Harmonious Partnerships

Finding balance in partnership and committed relationships while maintaining independence is an art that requires ongoing effort, understanding, and communication. It's an art that, when mastered, results in fulfilling, harmonious, and enduring partnerships. By nurturing individuality, promoting open communication, setting healthy boundaries, and prioritizing mutual support and trust, couples can enjoy the best of both worlds: the richness of partnership and the freedom of independence.

*The road to healing may be long,
but it's worth every step.*

Reflect & Pray

Father, I ask for wisdom to know how to balance my life, relationships, work, and ministry, with times of rest, relaxation, and recreation. Help me to make healthy choices.

> "Praise is my response while in the process."
> — Pastor Ken
>
> **TRUST THE PROCESS**

Chapter 9

THRIVING IN SINGLENESS

Singleness is not merely a transitional phase; it's a unique and valuable chapter of your life journey. In this chapter, we'll explore how to thrive in singleness, embracing the opportunities, strengths, and joys it offers.

Embracing the Present Moment

Thriving in singleness begins with embracing the present moment. Instead of viewing it as a period of waiting for something else, recognize that your life right now is full of possibilities, adventures, and growth.

Cultivating Self-Reliance

Singleness encourages self-reliance, which can be a profound source of empowerment. Embrace the opportunity to make decisions solely for yourself, take risks, and learn from both successes and setbacks.

Setting Personal Goals

Use your time in singleness to set and pursue personal goals with intention. Whether they are related to your career, personal growth, or hobbies, having clear goals gives your life direction and purpose.

Nurturing Self-Compassion

Self-compassion is especially important during times of singleness. Treat yourself caringly and avoid self-criticism. Understand that your worth is not defined by your relationship status but by your inherent value as a person.

Exploring Your Passions

Thriving in singleness often involves rediscovering and exploring your passions. Dive into activities and interests that bring you joy and fulfillment, and let your enthusiasm drive your personal growth.

Deepening Connections

Singleness doesn't mean isolation. Deepen your connections with trustworthy friends and family members. Invest time in nurturing those relationships and creating a support network that enhances your life.

Expanding Your Horizons

Use your singleness as an opportunity to expand your horizons. Travel, try new experiences, and embrace personal adventures. Those journeys can be rich sources of personal growth and self-discovery.

Giving Back to Others

Volunteering and contributing to communities through acts of kindness can provide a sense of fulfillment and purpose. It allows one to make a positive impact and enrich one's life through meaningful connections with others.

Singleness offers a unique opportunity for personal development. Invest in self-improvement, whether it's through education, therapy, or self-help resources. Continual growth enhances your well-being and adds depth to your life.

The Freedom of Choice

One of the most liberating aspects of singleness is the freedom of choice. Embrace this freedom as a chance to create the life you desire—one that aligns with your values, goals, and aspirations.

In the chapters ahead, we will delve deeper into the concept of thriving in singleness and explore how it can lead to a more fulfilling, purpose-driven life. Remember that your journey is not about waiting for someone else to complete you; it's about recognizing your completeness and celebrating the richness of the life you have the power to create.

Exploration of shifting mindsets to embrace the advantages of being single can lead to spiritual and personal growth:

The Power of Shifting Mindsets

Shifting our mindset to see the advantages of being single is a transformative journey. It's an opportunity to unlock spiritual and personal growth on a profound level. It challenges societal norms. Society often emphasizes the importance of romantic partnerships, marriage, and couples. Shifting our mindset challenges these norms and encourages us to find fulfillment in being single.

The Gift of Independence

Being single offers the gift of independence. It's a chance to make decisions, pursue dreams, and explore life without the need for compromise. Independence can lead to substantial personal growth. It encourages self-discovery, self-reliance, and self-confidence, all of which are vital for spiritual and personal development.

The Art of Self-Reflection

Being single provides ample time for self-reflection. This practice involves looking inward to understand your values, desires, strengths, and areas for growth.

Self-reflection fosters self-discovery and authenticity. It allows you to align your actions and decisions with your true self, promoting spiritual growth.

Cultivating Self-Love and Self-Care

Self-love is the cornerstone of spiritual and personal growth. Being single offers an ideal opportunity to nurture self-love by treating yourself with kindness, compassion, and respect. Self-care is a form of spiritual practice. Prioritize self-care routines, such as meditation, mindfulness, or yoga, to deepen your connection with yourself and the world around you.

Expanding Social Connections

Being single allows for the expansion of meaningful social connections. Nurture deep and meaningful friendships, as they can be a source of emotional support, shared experiences, and personal growth. We need support and inspiration during challenging times and moments of self-discovery. These relationships can contribute to our spiritual journey.

Pursuing Passion and Purpose

Passion fuels personal and spiritual growth. Being single grants the freedom to pursue your passions wholeheartedly, whether they are creative, career-oriented, or humanitarian. In the pursuit of passions, you may discover your life's purpose. This sense of purpose can be a guiding light on your spiritual journey.

Embracing Solitude as a Gift

Solitude is a gift often overlooked. It's a time to be alone with your thoughts, connect with your inner self, and deepen your spiritual understanding. Practice mindfulness during moments of solitude. It involves being fully present and aware of your thoughts and emotions. Mindfulness can lead to profound spiritual insights.

The Freedom of Choice

Being single grants the freedom of choice in every aspect of life. Embrace this freedom by making decisions that align with your values and aspirations. With freedom comes accountability and responsibility. Taking ownership of your choices fosters personal growth and spiritual maturity.

The Gift of Time and Energy

Being single provides the gift of time for self-improvement. Use this time to learn new skills, read, travel, or engage in personal development activities. Self-improvement is a gateway to spiritual growth. As you become a better version of yourself, you may find a deeper sense of purpose and meaning in your life.

Shifting our mindsets to see the advantages of being single is a transformative journey of self-discovery, spiritual growth, and personal development. It's an opportunity to embrace independence, cultivate self-love, expand social connections, pursue passions, and make choices that align with our authentic self. By recognizing the profound gifts that come with being single, we can embark on a path of growth and fulfillment that ultimately leads to a more meaningful and purposeful life.

I realize many of you have spent many days, weeks, months, and even years in disbelief that your relationship with your partner has come to an end, and it hurts to remember the memories, those melancholy moments, but know that the memories are additional gifts of your growing experiences and how far you have come. Look at it that way as you are going through the process.

The image of the pain as a deeply embedded thorn that requires tenderness and skill to remove is with you. It is a vivid reminder of how complex and wounded we are, and of our need to dig deeper to develop true compassion for ourselves as well as others. As the apostle Paul in the Bible reminds us, loving others requires us to be willing not only to "rejoice with those who rejoice," but to "mourn with those that mourn" (Rom 12:15). It requires all of us. In this very broken world, none of us escape unwounded. Hurt and scars are deeply embedded in each of us. But deeper still is the love we find in God's love, tender enough to draw out those thorns with the balm of compassion, willing to embrace both friend and enemy, to find healing together.

"The darkest night brings the brightest stars."
—John Green

Reflect & Pray

*Father, thank You for refining me while I walk the path of my singleness. While I am waiting for Your path of direction, help me to learn to love You so much, the way You love,
that it spills over into those around me.
I glorify You in this season of my life!*

> **Stop praying for an EXIT. Pray for endurance!**
> — Pastor Ken
>
> TRUST THE PROCESS

Chapter 10

ILLUMINATING FUTURE POSSIBILITIES

Future Possibilities

As you near the end of your journey of embracing solitude, it's time to cast your gaze toward the future. This chapter explores the infinite possibilities that await you, regardless of whether you choose to continue your path of solitude or embrace new horizons in your life.

The future is inherently uncertain, and that uncertainty can be both daunting and exhilarating. Instead of fearing the unknown, choose to embrace it as an opportunity for growth and adventure. Life's surprises can lead you to unexpected and beautiful places.

Regardless of your relationship status, you have the power to build a life filled with purpose. Define your values and passions and align your actions with them. A purpose-driven life is one that brings fulfillment and meaning.

Your journey of personal growth doesn't end with embracing solitude. Continue to evolve and learn about yourself. Explore new interests, seek out challenges, and cultivate a growth mindset that keeps you open to new possibilities.

As you move forward, dare to expand your dreams and aspirations. Allow yourself to imagine the life you truly desire, even if it seems out of reach. Your dreams can be powerful motivators for creating positive change.

Reevaluating Goals

Periodically reevaluate your goals and aspirations. As you gain new insights and experiences, your priorities may shift. Adapt your goals accordingly to ensure they remain aligned with your evolving sense of self.

Building Resilience

Life is filled with ups and downs, and building resilience is essential for navigating its challenges. Draw upon the strength you have cultivated on your journey of embracing solitude to face adversity with courage and determination.

Cultivating Relationships

If you choose to remain single or decide to pursue new relationships, prioritize cultivating healthy and meaningful connections with others. Cherish the people who bring positivity and love into your life.

Creating a Vision

Take time to create a vision for your future. Visualize the life you want to lead, the relationships you want to nurture, and the impact you want to make on the world. Your vision can serve as a guiding light on your journey.

Embracing the Present

While it's important to plan, remember to embrace the present moment. Life unfolds in the here and now, and the richness of your journey lies in each moment you live mindfully. As you look to the future, take a moment to celebrate how far you've come on your journey of embracing solitude. You've navigated the complexities of heartbreak, self-discovery, and personal growth, and you've emerged stronger and wiser.

In the chapters of your future, whether they are filled with solitude, new relationships, or a combination of both, know that you have the power to shape your destiny. Embrace the limitless possibilities that await you, for your journey is a testament to your resilience, strength, and capacity for growth.

The Power of Forward Thinking

Looking to the future is an act of embracing limitless possibilities and recognizing that old things have passed away. It's an invitation to build purposeful lives filled with growth, potential, and uncharted horizons.

Breaking Free from the Past
The past can hold us back with regrets, failures, and limitations. By shifting our focus to the future, we free ourselves from these constraints and open the door to boundless opportunities.

"Relationships are like glass. Sometimes it is better to leave them broken than hurt yourself trying to put it all back together." (Unknown)

Embracing Change and Transformation

Change is an inevitable part of life. Embracing the future means welcoming change with open arms, understanding that it brings growth and new experiences. Transformation is a process of shedding old layers and emerging as a better version of ourselves. It's a journey of self-discovery and self-improvement that propels us toward our purpose.

The Endless Possibilities Ahead

The future is a vast landscape of uncharted horizons. It holds countless possibilities that we have yet to explore. These possibilities are the canvas on which we can paint our purposeful lives. Our imagination and creativity are tools for unlocking these possibilities. They allow us to envision a future filled with innovation, invention, and personal fulfillment.

Building Purposeful Lives

Defining Your Purpose
Building a purposeful life begins with defining your purpose. What are your passions, values, and aspirations? Clarifying your purpose gives direction to your journey.

Aligning Actions with Purpose
Once you have defined your purpose, align your actions with it. Every decision and choice you make should reflect your commitment to living a purposeful life.

Setting Inspiring Goals

The Power of Goals
Setting inspiring goals is a crucial step in shaping your future. Goals provide motivation, focus, and a sense of achievement as you work toward them.

Short-Term and Long-Term Goals
Consider both short-term and long-term goals. Short-term goals offer quick wins and keep you motivated, while long-term goals give you a vision of where you want to be in the future.

The Role of Resilience

Resilience in the Face of Challenges
The journey toward a purposeful life is not without challenges. Resilience is the ability to bounce back from setbacks and continue moving forward.

Learning from Adversity
Adversity is usually a powerful teacher. Embrace challenges as opportunities for growth and learning. They often lead to insights and strengths you wouldn't have gained otherwise.

Expanding Horizons

To fully embrace the limitless possibilities of the future, be open to exploring new frontiers. This might involve stepping outside your comfort zone and taking calculated risks.

Global and Cultural Awareness
In a world filled with diverse cultures and perspectives, global and cultural awareness can broaden your horizons. It's an opportunity to learn from different traditions and values.

The Importance of Gratitude

Gratitude is a powerful mindset that enhances our appreciation for the future. Practice gratitude for the present moment and the opportunities ahead.

Fostering a Positive Outlook
A positive outlook on the future can significantly impact your journey. It attracts positivity, resilience, and the belief that you can overcome obstacles.

Nurturing Relationships and Connections

The Role of Relationships
Relationships play a vital role in building purposeful lives. Surround yourself with supportive, like-minded individuals who encourage your growth. Networking and collaboration can open doors to new possibilities. Engage with others who share your passions and interests, as they may offer valuable insights and opportunities.

Embracing Limitless Possibilities

Looking to the future with hope, determination, and a commitment to building purposeful lives is a transformative journey. It's an acknowledgment that the old things have passed away, making room for a brighter, more meaningful tomorrow. As you embrace the limitless possibilities ahead, remember that the power to shape your future lies within you. By setting inspiring goals, nurturing resilience, fostering gratitude, and developing meaningful relationships, you can create a future that aligns with your purpose and aspirations. The canvas is blank, and the possibilities are endless—now it's time to paint your masterpiece.

I ate Chinese food this evening as I began painting my masterpiece's ending. I normally don't pay attention to the fortune cookie, but this time I did. I cracked it open, and, within, the fortune stated, "Success is being at PEACE with yourself."

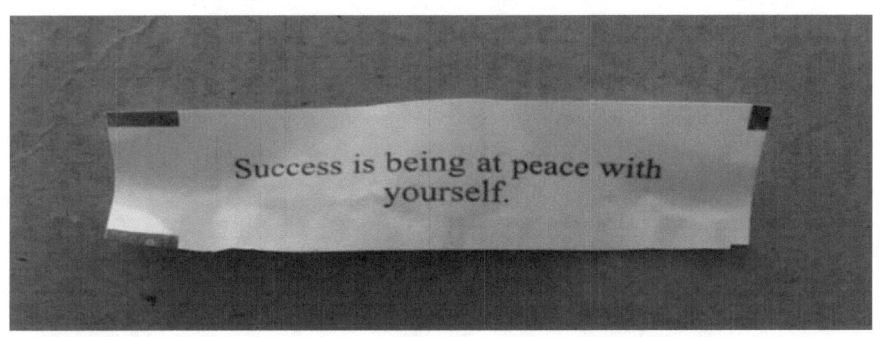

> Success is being at peace with yourself.

So, for those who have traveled to this point with me in this guide, I leave you with this.

"May the Master of Peace himself, always give you the gift of peace, always and in every way. The Lord be with all of you" (Excerpt 2 Thess 3:16, 18).

The Prince of Peace, who is peaceable Himself and the author of peace in all, requires peace, calls for it, and encourages it. By His presence, to comfort and refresh, by His power, to keep and preserve us, by His grace, to assist, and by His Spirit, to counsel, advise, as He directs us.

May your life be forever enriched by the wisdom, resilience, and boundless love that you've discovered along the way. Your journey continues, and the possibilities are infinite!

Blessings!!!

> **Real faith operates with missing information!**
>
> —Pastor Ken

TRUST THE PROCESS

CONCLUSION

Let us craft a conclusion that ties together the profound journey toward a fulfilling, progressive life, summarizing the essence of each of the ten chapters:

In the pages that have unfolded, we have embarked on an odyssey through the complexities of the heart, mind, and soul. Our journey has been both challenging and transformative, encompassing ten distinct chapters that have led us toward the radiant destination of illumination.

Chapter 1: The Journey of Self-Rediscovery

Our voyage commenced with the profound voyage of self-rediscovery. It reminded us that we are not defined solely by our relationships or past experiences. We learned to cherish our individuality, understanding that the foundation of any fulfilling life begins with a profound understanding of self.

Chapter 2: Healing from Heartbreak

Amid the journey, we faced heartbreak, a storm that tested our resilience. Yet, it's within the tempest of heartbreak that we discovered our own strength. We learned to rise, heal, and rebuild, recognizing that adversity is a catalyst for growth.

Chapter 3: The Power of Self-Love

Self-love became our guiding star, illuminating the path ahead. We discovered that to love another deeply, we must first love ourselves. This power sustained us, allowing us to nurture our own well-being and offer a love that's genuine and boundless.

Chapter 4: Reinventing Yourself

The blank canvas of reinvention beckoned, granting us the chance to rewrite our life's narrative. We embraced change, set new goals, and kindled the flames of resilience. Each day, we painted a new stroke, crafting a masterpiece of self-discovery.

Chapter 5: Navigating Loneliness

Loneliness, once a feared abyss, became a teacher. We learned that solitude is synonymous with isolation. In the quiet moments, we found the strength to listen to our hearts, to reflect, and to grow. Loneliness became an ally on our path to fulfillment.

Chapter 6: Dating Again – A New Adventure

Our journey took an exciting turn as we ventured into the realm of dating once more. We approached it with open hearts, armed with the wisdom and self-assurance gained from our previous chapters. Each date was an opportunity to learn, to connect, and to rediscover the beauty of human connection.

Chapter 7: Overcoming Relationship Baggage

We faced the shadows of our past, liberating ourselves from the weight of relationship baggage. Forgiveness became our armor, allowing us to move forward unburdened by the past. We discovered that by letting go, we made space for the light of the future to shine.

Chapter 8: Balancing Independence and Partnership

In our quest for fulfillment, we learned the delicate art of balance. Independence, cherished as a cornerstone of self-love, harmonized with the beauty of partnership. We found that a fulfilling life is one where we are both whole on our own and beautifully intertwined with another.

Chapter 9: Thriving in Singleness

We came to the reality that singleness doesn't mean isolation but a place of unique opportunity for personal development, and it offers the gift of independence as well as the freedom of choice in every aspect of life.

Chapter 10: Illuminating Future Possibilities

Singleness was no longer considered a waiting room but a destination of its own. It became a time of personal growth, self-care, and joy. Our eyes sparkled with anticipation as we gazed toward the horizon of future possibilities, knowing that a fulfilling life is a journey without end, marked by a continuous pursuit of self-discovery, love, and growth.

As we close the chapters of our journey, remember that solitude is not a static, lonely endeavor but an ongoing process. Embrace the lessons, the challenges, and the beauty of this ever-evolving voyage. They are all a part of the calculated steps designed by God.

"The steps of a good man/woman are ordered by the Lord. And he delighteth in his way. Though he/she falls, he shall not be utterly cast down. For the Lord upholdeth him with his hand" (Psalm 37:23-24).

Solitude is where we find our inner peace.

Reflect & Pray

*Father, thank You for Your peace,
the peace that surpasses all understanding!*

> "You'll never come out of a process empty-handed!
> — Pastor Ken
>
> **TRUST THE PROCESS**

AUTHOR PORTRAIT

A Tapestry of Inspiration

Dr. Sandra Hill is prevalently known in many communities, business marketplace, government, non-profits, ministerial circles, as well as political circles of civil rights. Once in blue moon, in the educational/university/civil rights arenas, you may hear someone say Dr. Hamilton; she is one in the same, that is her maiden name, so we introduce you to her here with that duality so there is no confusion if it's heard.

Dr. Sandra is a weaver of words who crafts narratives that resonate with the human soul. Her words are infused with empathy, insight, and an unwavering passion for guiding individuals toward self-rediscovery and healing.

Dr. Sandra has an introspective heart and an insatiable curiosity about the human experience. She possesses a unique ability to traverse the depths of the psyche. She delves into the intricate web of emotions, extracting truths that serve as lighthouses for those navigating the tumultuous seas of life.

Dr. Sandra's writing style is a testament to one of her gifts from God. It flows like a gentle stream, offering solace and wisdom, while at times surging like a mighty river, urging readers to embark on a daring journey of self-reinvention and growth. Her words are both a soothing balm and a call to action, each sentence carefully crafted to evoke introspection, empathy, and transformation.

It is not just words that define this author. It is her unwavering commitment to her readers. With every chapter, she extends a hand of motivation/guidance, a hand that has weathered its own storms of heartbreak and emerged stronger, ready to illuminate the path for others.

Dr. Sandra is not merely an observer of life; she is a participant in the human condition. Her journey of embracing solitude is not just a subject she writes about. It reflects her own experiences, triumphs, and lessons learned. It is a testimony of the power of resilience, self-love, and the relentless pursuit of fulfillment to a successful life.

In the pages she has crafted, she is a beacon of light and hope, a compassionate guide, and an advocate for the human spirit's boundless potential. Her words have the power to heal, to inspire, and to spark conversion. Through the chapters she reminds us that the journey is not solitary but a shared voyage, and she invites us to embark on this extraordinary odyssey together.

Bookings, Workshops, Conferences, Forums

Email: drsandrahill@yahoo.com
Email: drsandrahamilton@yahoo.com
Website: https://successfulreintegrations.org
Email: drshill@successfulreintegrations.org

RESOURCES

Cain, Susan. *Quiet: The Power of Introverts in a World that Can't Stop Talking.*

Cappiello, Robert Firpo. "Sounds of sorrow." *Brain & Life.* August/September 2023.

Goleman, Daniel. *Emotional Intelligence: Why It Can Matter More Than IQ.*

Harris, Michael: *The Gifts of Solitude: A Journey to Self-Discovery.*

Hicks, J.A. Schlegel, Arndt, J., & King, L.A. (2009). "Thine own self: True self-concept accessibility and meaning in life." *Journal of Personality and Social Psychology, 96*(2), 473–490.

International Journal of Environmental Research and Public Health (2023). "Symptoms of post-traumatic stress disorder in divorced individuals."

Shulman, Lisa M. *Before and After Loss: A Neurologist's Perspective on Loss, Grief, Our Brain.*

HOLY BIBLE — All scriptural references.

EMBRACING SOLITUDE

A GUIDE TO UNLOCKING GREATNESS IN THE PROCESS

In the quiet moments after the breakup of my marriage, when the echoes of shared laughter and the warmth of companionship faded into memories, I found myself standing on the threshold of a profound journey of self-rediscovery. Being in "singleness again" felt like uncharted territory, a land I never thought I would ever revisit. As I took my first steps, I soon realized that this journey had the potential to be something inordinate!

My book accounts for the fact that life has a way of knocking us down, sending our confidence levels plummeting. When at rock bottom, we tell ourselves we are not good enough, we are a loser, and we even make the mistake of comparing ourselves to others. Suddenly we begin to criticize everything about ourselves—our looks, our weight, our hair, our clothes, our walk, our talk—and no matter how hard we try, nothing feels right. Even the most confident person may have moments of insecurity, self-doubt, and self-loathing during those times.

Have you ever thought you were all alone with some of these critical feelings? Even losing faith? Think again. My book was written for those who have found themselves alone, lonely, and afraid.

- Are you trying to figure out who you are?
- Are you wondering what the next steps are in your life?
- Are you trying to navigate through painful challenges of loss?
- Have you found yourself in the realm of singleness, unraveling and shedding layers that no longer serve you?

In the cocoon of a relationship, it is easy to lose sight of who we are outside of that union. I have wrestled through almost all you can imagine. I have had plenty of obstacles, seasons of doubt, and dry spells. I have navigated through various periods of life: feeling rejected, disrespected, abandoned, like a failure, in pain, financially struggling, and then divorced. My book explores the intricacies of the learning experiences along my solitude voyage. It will dig into depths of emotions, navigate the challenges of letting go, and illuminate the path to moving forward. You are about to embark on a remarkable journey with me. It will inspire you. It will help you to rediscover your identity and help you to navigate through your many days and nights of feeling lost, lonely, and hopeless. I am praying that "Embracing Solitude" will be a blessing to you.

MEET THE AUTHOR

DR. SANDRA HILL

A woman of purpose with a nationwide mindset and many God-given gifts, including encouraging, teaching, leading, guiding, coaching, and ministering healing to others. She is a woman who remains grateful always for the things God has done in and through her life. It is her love language to see individuals inspired, empowered, and encouraged to live victorious, healed, progressive, and successful lives. She is an academician who holds a bachelor's degree in business administration (BBA), Master of Science degrees (Education/English/MRE), doctorates (Org Leader/Conflict Res), and Jacksonville Theological Seminary (Ministry). She is humbled to share a "small piece" of her with you!

PAGE INTENTIONALLY LEFT BLANK

PAGE INTENTIONALLY LEFT BLANK

PAGE INTENTIONALLY LEFT BLANK

PAGE INTENTIONALLY LEFT BLANK

PAGE INTENTIONALLY LEFT BLANK

PAGE INTENTIONALLY LEFT BLANK

Made in the USA
Columbia, SC
11 March 2025